ZERO PREP

Activities for Beginners

Ready-to-Go Activities for In-Person and Remote Language Teaching

2nd Edition

by

Laurel Pollard, Natalie Hess, Jan Heron, and Michal Marell

Zero Prep Activities for Beginners, Second Edition

Ready-to-Go Activities for In-Person and Remote Language Teaching

Copyright © 2023 by Pro Lingua Learning – Rockville, MD USA

The first edition of this book was originally published by Alta Book Center Publishers, San Francisco, California. This second edition has been revised and redesigned.

Credits:

Editor: **Michael C. Berman**

Cover Art and Book Design: **Laura Guzman Aguilar with Dani Joffré**

Interior Art: **Kathleen Peterson, Laura Guzman Aguilar, and Armin Castellón.**

PO Box 4467

Rockville, MD 20849 USA

Office: 301-424-8900

Orders: 800-888-4741

info@ProLinguaLearning.com

www.ProLinguaLearning.com

ISBN 978-0-86647-582-2

DEDICATIONS

Laurel dedicates this book

To my son Adam, my daughter Geneva, and my granddaughter Sedona: you are the reasons I want to live a long time and keep on growing. What a continuing delight it is to be in the world with you!

To dedicated teachers everywhere who could use a little more free time

Michal dedicates this book

To Jasmine and Ari, who always know how to make me smile

To my mother, who has always been my best friend and favorite teacher

Jan dedicates this book

To Suzannah, who thinks it's neat that her mom wrote a book

Acknowledgement

To Dr. Natalie Hess, who helped thousands of students and teachers become their best selves, and whose indispensable contributions made this book possible. Her influence continues to spread, a blessing to the world.

CONTENTS

INTRODUCTION 1

For Teachers Who Don't Have Time
to Read Introductions to New Books xii

INTRODUCTION 2

The Who, What, Why, and How of *Zero Prep for Beginners* xii

CHAPTER ONE: WARMUPS AND ICEBREAKERS

1.1   Hello! How Are You? 2

1.2   Early Bird Questions 2

1.3   Dance Party 3

1.4   One New Word 3

1.5   What's in My Wallet? 4

1.6   Checking the Weather 4

1.7   Taking Surveys 5

1.8   Offering Tea 6

1.9   What Day Is It Today? 6

1.10 What Can We Hear? 7

**You'll find more good warmups and icebreakers
in these other chapters:**

•   3.4   What's Your Name? Nice To Meet You! 23

•   3.5   Please and Thank You 23

CHAPTER TWO: LISTENING

2.1   Popcorn Listening 10

2.2   Singing Dictation: Building Up a Song 11

2.3   Using the Telephone 12

2.4   Let's Pack a Suitcase 13

2.5   Active True/False 14

2.6   Who Said It? 15

2.7   Catch the Teacher's Mistakes 16

2.8   Picture Dictation 17

2.9   Gossip 18

**You'll find more good listening activities
in these other chapters:**

•   1.7 Taking Surveys 5

•   1.9 What Day Is It Today? 6

•   3.6 Reading and Speaking 3 x 3 24

•   4.2 On the Wall Outside 31

•   7.1 Tell It Like It Isn't 76

CHAPTER THREE: SPEAKING

3.1   Classroom Language.. 20

3.2   What I Need 21

3.3   Reconstruct the Story 22

3.4   What's Your Name? Nice to Meet You!.................................... 23

3.5   Please and Thank You 23

3.6   Reading and Speaking 3 x 3 24

3.7   Let's Put on a Play! 26

3.8   Homework or Quiz Review: Seek and Find 27

3.9   What I Eat, What You Eat.. 28

**You'll find more good speaking activities
in these other chapters:**

- 2.3 Using the Telephone 12
- 2.9 Gossip 18
- 4.2 On the Wall Outside 31
- 4.6 Add a Picture 36
- 6.5 Practicing Counting 59
- 6.18 Use it Before I Sleep 72
- 7.1 Tell It Like It Isn't 76
- 7.7 Building Dialogues About Food 83
- 7.11 Playing with Wh-Questions 87
- 7.12 Think Fast! Practicing Verb Tenses 88
- 7.13 This is My Elephant 89
- 7.14 Weekly Routines 90
- 7.18 When Suddenly 94

CHAPTER FOUR: READING

4.1 Let's Make it False 30

4.2 On the Wall Outside 31

4.3 Dictocomp: Rewriting from Key Words 33

4.4 Students Choose Who's Next 34

4.5 New Words and What They Mean 35

4.6 Add a Picture 36

4.7 Predicting from the Title 37

4.8 Predicting from the Picture 37

4.9 Telling Back and Forth 38

**You'll find more good reading activities
in these other chapters:**

- 2.6   Who Said It? 15
- 2.7   Catch the Teacher's Mistakes 16
- 3.6   Reading and Speaking 3 x 3 24
- 3.7   Let's Put on a Play! 26
- 5.1   Let's Learn Those Letters 42
- 6.2   TPR: Making a Peanut Butter Sandwich 56
- 7.16 Scrambling Words in a Sentence 92

CHAPTER FIVE: WRITING

5.1   Let's Learn Those Letters 42

5.2   Fill-in the-Blank Dictation 43

5.3   Let's Find Some Useful Mistakes 44

5.4   Chain Story 45

5.5   The Appearing and Disappearing Sentence 46

5.6   The Vocabulary of Sentences and Paragraphs 46

5.7   Partners in Writing 48

5.8   Editing and Revision: I Can Do It Myself 49

5.9   Spelling Improvement 51

5.10 One-Minute Feedback 51

**You'll find more good writing activities
in these other chapters:**

- 3.8   Homework or Quiz Review: Seek and Find 27
- 6.7   Vocabulary Cards 61
- 6.11 Alphabet on the Wall: Collecting Words 65

CHAPTER SIX: VOCABULARY

6.1   Classic Total Physical Response (TPR):

       Actions Tell the Story 54

6.2   TPR: Making a Peanut Butter Sandwich 56

6.3   TPR: Working with Money 57

6.4   From Pictures to Words 58

6.5   Practicing Counting 59

6.6   Getting to Know You: A Birthday Game 60

6.7   Vocabulary Cards 61

6.8   Half a Picture 62

6.9   All the Words We Know 63

6.10   Manipulating Objects or Pictures 64

6.11   Alphabet on the Wall: Collecting Words 65

6.12   Two Unrelated Pictures: How Are They the Same?..................... 66

6.13   The Hokey Pokey 67

6.14   Playing with Numbers: What Adds Up to 14?.......................... 68

6.15   Playing with Numbers: Students Make Their Own Equations ... 69

6.16   What We Already Know About This..................................... 70

6.17   Four Corners Vocabulary 71

6.18   Use it Before I Sleep 72

6.19   What Am I Drawing? 72

6.20   Student-Run Vocabulary Review 73

6.21   Creating New Stories with Our Words 74

**You'll find more good vocabulary activities
in these other chapters:**

- 1.7 Taking Surveys 5
- 2.1 Popcorn Listening.. 10
- 2.4 Let's Pack a Suitcase 13
- 2.8 Picture Dictation 17
- 3.2 What I Need 21
- 4.5 New Words and What They Mean 35
- 7.1 Tell It Like Isn't 76
- 7.6 Truth or Chair? 81
- 7.9 Cleaning Up the Mess 85
- 7.10 What Kind of Noun is This? 86
- 7.13 This is My Elephant 89

CHAPTER SEVEN: GRAMMAR

7.1 Tell It Like It Isn't... 76

7.2 Make Questions for the Answers 77

7.3 Sentence Expansion 78

7.4 Sentence Contraction 79

7.5 Substitution Drills 80

7.6 Truth or Chair?.. 81

7.7 Building Dialogues About Food 83

7.8 What Do We Do? Practicing Short Answers with Do and Does ... 84

7.9 Cleaning Up the Mess... 85

7.10 What Kind of Noun is This? 86

7.11 Playing with Wh-Questions 87

7.12 Think Fast! Practicing Verb Tenses 88

7.13 This is My Elephant.. 89

7.14 Weekly Routines 90

7.15 Preposition Pictures 91

7.16 Scrambling Words in a Sentence 92

7.17 Vocabulary Chain 93

7.18 When Suddenly 94

**You'll find more good grammar activities
in these other chapters:**

* 1.7 Taking Surveys 5

* 2.1 Popcorn Listening 10

* 2.8 Picture Dictation 17

* 5.4 Chain Story 45

* 5.5 The Appearing and Disappearing Sentence 46

* 5.8 Editing and Revision: I Can Do It Myself! 49

* 6.10 Manipulating Objects or Pictures 64

* 6.19 What Am I Drawing? 72

INDEX OF ACTIVITY FUNCTIONS/TOPICS

1. Assessment: Error Correction 95

2. Community-Building Activities 95

3. Dialogues 96

4. Drawing... 96

5. Energizers 96

6. Feedback Built into the Lesson 97

7. First Few Days 97

8. Grammar 97

9. High Beginners 98

10. Low Beginners 99

11. Movement 99

12. Multiple Intelligences 100

13. Music and Song 100

14. Pictures... 101

15. Polite Phrases 101

16. Preview 101

17. Pronunciation 102

18. Review 102

19. Settling Down the Class 102

20. Short Activities.. 102

21. Spelling 103

22. Students Helping Students 103

23. Students in Charge of Their Own Learning 103

24. Vocabulary Categories 104

ALPHABETICAL INDEX OF ACTIVITIES 106

INTRODUCTION 1

For Teachers Who Don't Have Time to Read Introductions to New Books

What if you reviewed every activity for beginning students you ever used or heard of and chose only activities that are the very best ones for language learning?

What if you then selected from that collection only those activities that take no time for the teacher to prepare?

And finally, what if you chose from the remaining collection only those activities which can be delivered both in-person and online?

We did that.

Here it is.

Enjoy!

INTRODUCTION 2

The Who, What, Why, and How of Zero Prep Activities for Beginners

Who is this book for?

Let's face it: teachers of beginners are often underserved. We know because we have been there: you find a book or an online resource that promises it's for beginners, then have to spend too much time adapting it for your students. This collection is the fruit of years of collaborating with teachers to provide strategies that work in our multi-level beginner classes.

Zero Prep for Beginners is for any teacher who has ever had too much to do and too little time:

- veteran teachers who want more proven strategies that help beginning students learn — and remember what they've learned.

- new teachers, volunteers, and substitutes who need a repertoire of effective beginning-level activities fast. These include the strategies and techniques the authors wish we'd had when we were starting to teach. They work. Students learn. You can feel good about your teaching from the start!

These activities are suitable for teaching not just English, but any language. For the sake of convenience, the examples are in English.

Content-area teachers in diverse settings use Zero Prep, too! Whatever the subject matter, ALL classrooms use language, and these activities and strategies are at the core of good teaching.

What's special about beginners?

The activities in this book have been carefully developed to help address the needs particular to beginning language students.

1. Beginners need plenty of input. They cannot yet create new language, but they can recreate and reformulate language that they encounter. The activities in *Zero Prep for Beginners* give you many ways to provide meaningful language input, including routines for using readings, dictations, pictures, actions, and songs.

2. Beginners need a great deal of repetition. Have you ever lamented, "But I just taught this last week!" This can happen because we didn't want our students to get bored, so we moved on too quickly. For long-term learning, beginners need a lot of repetition — more than many of us realize. So relax and rely on your students; they are our best guides about when they want to practice more and when they're ready to move on.

3. Beginners need a lot of support, more than the teacher alone can provide. These carefully structured activities provide that support. In addition, you'll find pair and group designed to help beginners move toward independence and experience the thrill of "I can do it myself!"

4. Beginners often worry too much about making mistakes because everything in the new language is a mystery at first. There are several ways we can support our students in getting past this fear.

   • One way is to help them feel safe. For example, we can be careful not to overcorrect. Learning is an organic process, not a series of perfect performances. Students also feel safer as they realize that their teacher and classmates know and like them. (See the list of "Class Cohesion" activities in the Index of Activity Functions.)

   • Another way is to praise useful mistakes. When we thank our students for the errors they make on "the edge of learning," they are more willing to take risks. Instead of being afraid of mistakes, they learn to make them cheerfully. Everyone learns together in the process. You will find this tip in many activities throughout the book.

   • A third strategy for dealing with mistakes is to encourage students to correct themselves. It is tempting to jump in and help, but we must be sure not to do too much for them. We can give them good "shoes," but they need to do the walking themselves. The peer-checking and self-checking activities in *Zero Prep for Beginners* develop students' own correctness monitors, so they make fewer habitual errors and take charge of their own learning. See "Editing and Revision: I Can Do It Myself!" (Chapter 5, page 49).

   • Finally, we can reduce our own anxiety about our students' mistakes by using activities that ensure correctness. See "Telling Back and Forth," (Chapter 4, page 38), for one of many activities that provide enough support for everyone to practice the language correctly.

Why did we write this book?

Especially at the beginning levels, we teachers often work harder than we need to or should. There is no end of need around us, and our profession draws people who feel that being "good" means working ever harder to help everyone — often without enough institutional support. When we feel rushed and tired, we lose some of our awareness, flexibility, and creativity. Students inevitably notice. Enjoyment ebbs. Burnout looms. Students learn less. And all, ironically, because we tried so hard.

Yet the essence of a successful classroom lies in having students do the work while the teacher facilitates. These meticulously curated Zero Prep activities allow the teacher to do just that, and to teach better – more engagingly, inclusively, and energetically – in the process.

Writing this book reminded us why we love teaching at the beginning levels: with activities like these, students see their progress week by week. They get excited, and so do we!

A Crucial Distinction: Not "Zero Planning," but "Zero Prep"

We distinguish between **PLANNING** — the vision we have of our students' goals and how to help them get there, and **PREPARATION** — the busy-work we do before, during, and after class.

Here are a few examples of "prep": Do you spend time

*   going through readings to find words that may be new to your students?
*   preparing comprehension questions?
*   creating variations for multi-level classes?
*   correcting errors in sets of papers?
*   deciding how to engage multiple intelligences?

This collection provides you Zero Prep ways of doing all these tasks and more!

When we incorporate these strategies into our lessons, we spend much less time on the repetitive chores of preparation. The result: planning becomes easier because we have time to relax, observe, reflect, and recover our vision. We find that we're teaching better and enjoying it more!

Highly Adaptable Activities

A unique feature of this book is that it showcases highly adaptable activities.

That is, the strategies built into these activities are so effective, so flexible, that we find ourselves using the activity again and again, varying the content and level but keeping the basic steps intact. When students have done an activity before, they feel more secure. They can plunge right in, giving all their attention to the task and the language without needing to figure out what they're supposed to do.

These strategies — specifically tailored for beginning levels — include choral repetition, special tips for mingles and group work, ways to use their new language outside class, and teaching "buddies" how to coach a classmate who needs help.

What makes this book so easy to use?

The whole point here is to save you time, so we are not going to recommend that you read this book from cover to cover. Instead, use the chapter titles and — even more helpful — the indexes, to find the activities you need.

Our chapter titles guide you to activities for the four skills of listening, speaking, reading, and writing, as well as icebreakers, vocabulary, and grammar.

But that's not enough. Too often, we teachers find a book that we know will help us, but it stays on the shelf because we don't have time to explore it. We've designed Zero Prep's indexes to take you directly to what you need now, for the class that starts in half an hour. You'll find, for instance, activities that energize your class / settle it down / preview or review material / build classroom community and trust / put students in charge of their own learning / provide instant feedback about correctness during a lesson / and so on. Reading through the indexes at the back is the best way to get started using the book!

We recommend adding one Zero Prep activity at a time to your repertoire. After you've used it three times, you and your students will know whether it suits you. It won't be long before you realize that your teaching life has changed for the better and your students are learning more!

Some Basic Terminology of Remote/Online Teaching

- Breakout rooms: These are a way for you to put students in pairs or small groups. You can put specific students into a breakout room, or you can randomly assign students to breakout rooms.
- Shuffle the breakout room: Move students into new breakout rooms to work with a different partner or group.
- Main room: This is the space where the class is all together. You will see an icon for each student. If they have their camera on, you will be able to see their faces.
- Raised-hand icon: Students click on this reaction icon to show that they are raising their hand.
- Poll: Use a poll to have students answer brief surveys.
- Discussion board: When students post on a discussion board, everyone can see what they post. They can comment on their classmate's post on the discussion board.

The Two Books in the Zero Prep Series

We created *Zero Prep for Beginners* because we recognized that the needs of students at the beginning level are unique and require different approaches. We knew that this population of students (and their teachers) needed an entire book solely devoted to them!

Our companion book, *Zero Prep for All Levels*, on the other hand, addresses the full range of students' needs, providing activities for all levels of your curriculum.

Supercharge Your Teaching!

Are you looking for ways to fine-tune classic teaching strategies like brainstorming, mingles, pair work, and small group work? Would you like to see a collection of classic classroom management tips? Could you use some more timesaving strategies across all the language skills?

You will spot some of these in the book. To download the full set, see our free guide *Supercharge Your Teaching* on our website: ProLingualLearning.com/resources.

A Final Word to Our Colleagues

Not every activity needs to be zero prep. But teachers all over the world have told us that incorporating these activities into their lessons restores the joy to teaching and gives them more free time to call an old friend, plan a dinner party, relax with a good book, or go for a walk.

We are delighted to have updated *Zero Prep for Beginners* for you.

We remain passionate about our own teaching and passionate about you. Our students need us relaxed and creative. So do our families, our friends, and the world. We hope this approach to teaching will be as transformative for you as it has been for us and for thousands of teachers worldwide.

Chapter One

Warmups and Icebreakers

Why do we need warmups and icebreakers? They transition students into the target language at the start of class and help them get to know one another, creating a trusting and supportive class environment.

At the beginning level, many students are filled with enthusiasm as they explore a new language. Other students may enter the target language reluctantly. All students have days when they feel uncertain about how to use this language, and that may be even more true at the beginning levels. They may become tense and fearful, just when they should allow themselves to become relaxed risk-takers.

These activities help with that! They are non-threatening and fun and will even motivate students to be on time for class!

1.1 HELLO! HOW ARE YOU?

Basic greetings are very helpful for beginning students. Here's an easy way to practice them as students enter class.

 AIMS: Learning the vocabulary of greetings, building classroom community

Procedure:

1. Write on the board some words or phrases people use to greet one another. For example, you might write

   A. "Hi." / "Good morning." / "Good afternoon." / "How are you?"

   B. "Fine, thanks!" / "I'm OK." / "Not so good today."

2. Model these as students enter the class and encourage them to circulate and greet their classmates.

   > Online: Students greet one another as they join the class.

1.2 EARLY BIRD QUESTIONS

Students often encounter words, idioms, or situations outside class that they don't understand about their target language and its culture. This icebreaker offers them a reason to come to class on time or a bit early.

 AIM: Answering students' real-life questions

Procedure:

1. Students who arrive early share something they encountered that they don't understand. This might be a single word or a situation.

2. Write these on the board. You or classmates offer help.

3. Move on to your planned lesson.

> This activity works equally well in an online class with no adaptations.

> **Supercharge Your Teaching!**
>
> Many of us have found a way to make our board work more effective. For more information, see "Look Back at the Board Before Erasing" in our free guide *Supercharge Your Teaching*, downloadable from ProLinguaLearning.com/resources.

1.3 DANCE PARTY

In many cultures, a party's not a party unless there's dancing! It's easy to bring that energy into our classes, energizing our bodies and waking up our brains. Every culture, and every student, will have their own ways of moving to music, so don't be shy! Students are delighted with whatever moves we make as we join the fun.

You can use "Dance Party" at the start of class to set a lively tone, or whenever the class seems bored or anxious, or as a reward at the end of class.

 AIMS: Energizing the class, sharing music from various cultures
MATERIALS: Your favorite dance music to play in class

Procedure:

1. At the start of class, surprise your students by playing your dance music. Start moving to the rhythm a bit and invite them to stand up and join you. Dance together for a little while, just for fun.

2. Invite students to find good dance music. It might be from their home culture, the culture of their target language, or any music that makes them feel like dancing. Ask for a volunteer and name a day when they will lead the dance party.

3. On that day, invite the student to share their music and let the dancing begin!

4. When you've danced enough, go on to your lesson plan – or send everyone out dancing at the end of class. Do this with different students' music as often as you like.

> This activity works equally well in an online class with no adaptations.

1.4 ONE NEW WORD

It's important to help students recognize that they are learning their target language outside of class as well as inside. This activity lets students show off their new vocabulary and encourages the whole class to share.

 AIM: Expanding vocabulary

Procedure:

1. As students enter the class, encourage volunteers to tell you one word they recently learned outside of class.

2. Write this word on the board and help the student explain to the class how they learned it.

> This activity works equally well in an online class with no adaptations.

1.5 WHAT'S IN MY WALLET?

Real objects always make an activity more interesting! Here, students handle and name the objects they carry with them.

AIMS: Expanding vocabulary about common items, getting to know classmates
MATERIALS: Items in your pockets, wallet, or purse. Students will have their own items.

Procedure:

1. Show a few of the items you carry with you. Write the items' names on the board and say a few words about each. When possible, demonstrate appropriate actions with them.

2. In small groups, students do the same. If students don't have the words they need, they can visit another group or the teacher to ask for help.

> Online: Put a small group in each breakout room. Students can send a message to you in the chat if they need help.

3. Back together as a class, volunteers may share one interesting item they saw. The possibilities for vocabulary expansion are vast and lead to common, high-interest words.

> Online: Students return to the main room before sharing.

1.6 CHECKING THE WEATHER

Everyone talks about the weather. This activity offers great speaking practice for low-beginning students, who need more repetition than many of us realize.

 AIM: Teaching vocabulary about the weather

Procedure:

1. Say, "Let's look at the weather today." Go to the window and describe today's weather.

2. Repeat what you said as you write on the board sentences such as "It's warm. It's a nice day. The sun is shining."

3. Ask a student, "What is the weather like today?" After the student responds, encourage the class to repeat the answer chorally. Do this for several more rounds if it seems productive.

Extension: After your students are familiar with this routine, you might ask them, "What do you think the weather is like in your home country today?"

> This activity works equally well in an online class with no adaptations.

1.7 TAKING SURVEYS

This speaking activity helps students to get to know one another. It generates a lot of useful words because the content comes from students' own lives. This activity is marvelously flexible: beyond helping students get to know one another, you can use it to teach or review other content material by changing the categories on the chart.

 AIMS: Practicing information questions, speaking in complete sentences, getting to know classmates

Procedure:

1. Draw the following table on the board. Here are some headings you might choose.

Name of Student	Favorite Food	Favorite Place	Favorite Singer	Favorite Thing to Do for Fun	Favorite School Subject

2. Students copy it, listing classmates' names in the first column.

3. Teach any unknown words in the chart.

4. For each heading, students practice the following question chorally: "What is your favorite ___?"

5. Students mingle to interview classmates. They should ask each partner only one question, say "Thank you, ____," write that one answer, and then move on to another classmate. The idea is to mingle. They may return to a classmate several times.

> Online: Put a few students in each breakout room. After a short time, shuffle the breakout rooms.

6. Circulate, helping out with vocabulary and speaking as needed. Encourage students to ask complete questions, not just point to a blank or say a single word.

7. Continue as long as interest is high. The charts don't have to be completely filled.

8. Students return to their seats with their charts. Ask, "Who knows what Alia's favorite food is?"

> Online: Students return to the main room before sharing.

9. Volunteers answer. Write useful words on the board as they come up. Students listen carefully and fill in more blanks in their own charts.

1.8 OFFERING TEA

In many cultures, people share a cup of tea before doing business. Here's a way to evoke the warm, trusting feelings that come with this tradition.

 AIMS: Establishing a personal relationship with students, learning vocabulary about beverages

MATERIALS: A container with something to drink; glasses or cups to serve your students

Procedure:

1. From time to time, pour tea or juice for your students as they enter class. You might tell them you're doing this in case they might be thirsty. It's an easy, tangible way to show your students that you care about them.

   > Online: Give students a few minutes to get something to drink. They hold their beverages up to the camera to show what they're drinking.

2. Ask students, "What do you usually drink at home?" Facilitate a brief discussion of their cultural traditions and what they like to drink.

Variation: In later classes, students may volunteer to bring a refreshing drink to share with classmates.

1.9 WHAT DAY IS IT TODAY?

This activity creates a classroom ritual and establishes a friendly and supportive classroom community. You may want to do this every day until students master basic calendar language.

 AIMS: Reviewing days of the week, months of the year, and seasons of the year; reviewing numbers; establishing classroom ritual

MATERIALS: A large calendar

Procedure:

1. Place a large calendar in the front of the class.

   > Online: Share your screen to show a calendar.

2. Ask the class to repeat the days of the week (or the months or the seasons) after you.

3. Ask, "What day is it today?" "What day was it yesterday?" "What day will it be tomorrow?" After each question, a volunteer answers and the class repeats chorally.

Variation:

- Use months instead of days by asking, "What month is it now? What number is this month in the year?" Elicit several correct responses. Insist on ordinal numbers, for example: "the third month, the sixth month."
- Use seasons by asking, "What season is this?" and "What is your favorite season?"

1.10 WHAT CAN WE HEAR?

Students need to transition from the multiple stimulations of life outside class and get ready to learn. Focusing full attention on one thing at the beginning of class can help! "What Can We Hear?" captures students' interest because they hear more than they thought they could! You can also use it any time you want to rein in the energy level.

 AIMS: Learning vocabulary to describe common sounds, calming the energy level of a class, focusing attention on listening

Procedure:

1. Students listen silently for two minutes, noticing everything they can hear inside the classroom.

2. As a class, students tell what they heard. If they don't have the words they need, they may say it in their native language, draw it, imitate it, or use other ways to express it.

3. Classmates confirm if they also heard that sound and mention more sounds they heard.

4. Teach vocabulary as it comes up and congratulate students for how much they heard.

> Online: Every student will hear different sounds and can share what they heard.

5. (Optional) As a class, students may make vocabulary cards for one or two of the most valuable words. (See "Vocabulary Cards" on page 61.)

Variation: On other days, students listen for sounds outside the class.

Chapter Two

Listening

It's not easy to understand what we hear in a new language. Everything may sound like a noisy stream with no breaks and no meaning. This is isolating at first. Then gradually we recognize a word here and there, then a sentence, then miraculously a whole conversation.

Our students need to understand their teacher, friends, boss, neighbors, clerks, and officials. They also want to understand songs and other kinds of entertainment.

Our students need plenty of time to practice their listening skills so these sounds take on meaning. The activities in this chapter will help your students join the world of spoken words.

2.1 POPCORN LISTENING

Popcorn Listening isn't meant to be a comprehension activity; instead, students focus on listening for particular words. This simple activity has many benefits! It helps beginners distinguish words in a stream of sound. Depending on the words you choose to focus on, students might pay attention to unstressed words like articles, prepositions, and the short conjunctions; students often miss or misuse these words in their writing because they don't hear them in speech. On another day, you might focus on sight-sound correspondences by choosing words with a sound your students are learning to spell.

Another plus: Popcorn Listening gives everyone a chance to stand up and sit down again quickly several times, which pumps oxygen to the brain. It's fun! As students see their classmates popping up and down, they often start laughing.

AIMS: Helping beginners distinguish words in a stream of sound, energizing the class, teaching parts of speech holistically (see note below)

SETUP: Choose several words you want to focus on from a text students are familiar with

Procedure:

1. Write on the board a set of words that you have chosen and assign a word to each student. It's OK to give the same word to more than one student. Each student writes their word on a piece of paper. If they're not sure what their word means, they can get help from other students or from you.

2. Tell students, "I'm going to read to you now. Each time you hear your word, stand up and sit down quickly." Have students sit on the edge of their chairs. Demonstrate by reading a couple of sentences so some students show how to stand and sit quickly for their word.

3. Read the passage out loud. Don't pause on the words you've handed out; as soon as each student hears their word, they stand up and sit right back down again.

4. Read the passage a few more times. Students often laugh; watching their friends pop up and down is fun!

> This activity works equally well in an online class with no adaptations.

Note: Want to teach parts of speech? Do a short Popcorn Listening every day for a couple of weeks, choosing only nouns. Students get a thorough sense of what a noun is, what it does, the forms it can take, and where it occurs in sentences! Then for a couple of weeks, have students stand only for verbs every day. Later, move on to other parts of speech.

2.2 SINGING DICTATION: BUILDING UP A SONG

People remember songs they learned long ago, even when many other things are forgotten. For language learners, songs carry grammar, vocabulary, idioms, culture — all the richness of their target language — deep into memory.

One easy way to bring the power and the joy of song into our classrooms is to have students build up a song with choral repetition, line by line. Even people who think they don't like to sing enjoy this activity. Not even the teacher needs to sing well!

 AIMS: Listening to a song, improving pronunciation and spelling, learning vocabulary and grammar holistically

Procedure:

1. Choose a short song you know well. Display or distribute the lyrics to students.

2. Sing the first line. Students sing it back to you together. Work on pronunciation of important sounds if needed. Repeat until most students are singing it confidently.

   Note: You can play the song if you do not feel comfortable singing.

   > Online: If some students are distracted by connectivity or lag problems, they listen when the teacher is singing and may turn down their sound when the class is singing. The activity is still worthwhile.

3. Continue by singing the first and second lines. Students sing them back.

4. Sing the first, second and third lines. Continue to build up the song in this way until the class is singing the whole song.

Extension:

Students may write as much as they can remember of the song, then compare with what classmates have written or with the lyrics you showed earlier. For fun, you can sing the song together one more time.

> Online: Put a pair in each breakout room if they are comparing with a classmate.

Supercharge Your Teaching!

It's not always easy to know when students are ready for the next step in our lesson. For some good tips, see "Who's Ready to Move On?" in our free guide *Supercharge Your Teaching*, downloadable from ProLinguaLearning.com/resources.

2.3 USING THE TELEPHONE

Talking on the telephone frightens most beginning students. This activity will help them become more comfortable on the telephone.

AIMS: Practicing telephone conventions, making an appointment

SETUP: For online classes, post the conversation from Step 1 on your course site.

Procedure:

1. Display a short telephone conversation like the one below. Using choral repetition, practice it with the whole class.

    A: Hello?

    B: Hello, this is _____ (their own name). May I speak to _____ (the name of the person who just answered)?

    B: This is _____.

    A: Oh, hi_____. Can you meet me for lunch today?

    B: Sure, ___(caller's name). I'll be glad to. Let's meet at the cafe at 12 o'clock.

    A: Great! See you then.

    B: Goodbye.

    A: Bye!

2. To demonstrate what students will do in pairs, call on a volunteer. Pick up an imaginary phone and hold it to your ear. Pretend to dial the number and say, "Ring, ring." The student says, "Hello?" You continue the conversation in the role of B above.

3. After the end of the conversation, choose a new volunteer. This time, the student calls you on their imaginary phone, and you take the role of A above.

4. Put students in pairs to practice the conversation. Students mingle to find new partners often. Make sure they practice sometimes in the A role and sometimes as B.

    Online: Put pairs in breakout rooms. Shuffle the breakout rooms several times.

5. (Optional) If some students have made an actual appointment, they can share this experience with the class.

    Online: Students return to the main room before sharing.

Extension: Students may change the meeting place and the time. Once they've mastered this, you may vary the content of the conversation endlessly depending on what your class needs to practice. For example, practice calling a doctor's office to make an appointment.

2.4 LET'S PACK A SUITCASE

Students often need to put items in a suitcase, put food in a grocery cart, or furnish an apartment. In this adaptable actvity, they listen carefully to their teacher and classmates as they practice vocabulary sets of personal items. The example below is about packing a suitcase.

AIM: Expanding vocabulary of common personal items

SETUP: Photocopy the illustrations below and cut them apart, making sure that there is at least one travel item for each member of your class. It is fine for two or three students to have the same travel item.

> Online: Scan the illustrations and post them on your course site.

cowboy hat   cap   warm hat   shirt

t-shirt   tank top   sweatshirt   jacket

coat   pants   jeans   shorts

bathrobe   sweater   sock   boot   shoe

comb   toothbrush   brush   shampoo   flashlight   book

sunglasses   passport

Procedure:

1. Ask students to imagine that the class will be going on a trip and we have to pack a suitcase. Gesture to an imaginary suitcase on your desk.

2. Call on a student and give them a picture of a coat, for example. Write "coat" on the board and say, "This is the coat we will need in our suitcase. Kumiko has the coat."

> Online: Share your screen to show the picture of the coat. Call on one student and say, "Kumiko, you're going to have the coat. Write this word down so you remember it."

3. Continue handing out items to students until everyone has something.

4. Now it's time to start packing your suitcase. Say, "I need a _____ in my suitcase. Who has a _____?" Encourage volunteers to say, "Kumiko has the coat."

5. A student with this item comes up and puts it in your suitcase. Thank the student warmly.

6. Continue collecting items until you have them all in your suitcase.

Extension: For any group of items students might need to gather in real life, find a set of illustrations to practice with. You might play with items to furnish a house or food to put in a grocery cart. Vary the dialogue depending on whether the students are talking to a salesperson, friend, or family member who is helping them.

2.5 ACTIVE TRUE/FALSE

This is a great way to assess students' recall of a text they have read, as well as their listening skills. It gets them up and moving, which energizes everyone!

AIMS: Listening closely, checking reading and listening comprehension, energizing the class

MATERIALS: A passage students have read

Procedure:

1. Post the word "True" on one side of the room and the word "False" on the other side of the room. On the wall between the two, post a note saying, "Please repeat the sentence."

> Online: Set up a poll with "True" and "False" as options.

2. All students stand in the middle of the room. Say, "I am going to read sentences from our reading. Some of my sentences will be true, and some will be false. If the sentence is true, run and stand under the word "True." If it is false, run and stand under the word "False." If you aren't sure, stand under the "Please Repeat" sign.

> Online: Tell students to indicate their answers on the poll. Instruct them to send you a message in the chat if they need you to repeat the sentence.

Procedure (continued):

3. Read sentences from the text, changing some words to make false statements. Stop after each sentence as students run and stand where they want to be.

    > Online: Students indicate their answer on the poll.

4. If anyone is standing under the "Please Repeat" sign, read the sentence again until they move to the "True" or "False" sign.

    > Online: If you receive a message in the chat, repeat the sentence until everyone has chosen true or false.

5. Read the original sentence to show which group is correct. You may want students to repeat this chorally.

6. Students move back to the middle of the room to hear the next statement and choose their positions. Repeat until you have finished the text.

Note: Encourage students to think for themselves, not just follow the crowd. Tell them to stand up for what they believe is correct, even if they are standing alone!

2.6 WHO SAID IT?

Beginning language learners understand much more than they can express. Here's a task that gives them plenty to read and listen to, then allows them to demonstrate their comprehension with one-word answers.

AIMS: Listening carefully, reviewing a reading or listening text, demonstrating comprehension

MATERIALS: A story students have already worked with

Procedure:

1. Choose a story your students have already listened to or read.

2. Say something one character said (or might have said). For example, say, "Please let me go to the dance!"

3. Ask the class, "Who said it?"

4. Students quickly decide on a response. Call on one student to answer. They may call out, "Cinderella!" If this is correct, the class repeats, "Cinderella!" If a student answers incorrectly, call on other students until you hear a correct answer for the class to repeat.

5. Continue with more questions.

> This activity works equally well in an online class with no adaptations.

2.7 CATCH THE TEACHER'S MISTAKES

When we make intentional mistakes as we read aloud, students stay alert as they listen! This activity also allows for a bit of role reversal as they interrupt you to correct your "mistakes."

Another benefit: students are often shy about asking a speaker to repeat something they didn't understand. This activity makes it easier for them to interrupt because they know that the error is not in their listening ability but in what you just said.

Finally, beginners need a lot of input. When we read aloud to our class as they follow along in their book, we are helping them with intonation, pronunciation, and spelling/sound correspondences.

AIMS: Listening for mistakes, interrupting, asking for clarification
MATERIALS: A reading students already understand well

Procedure:

1. Choose a familiar passage to read aloud to your class.

2. Tell students that sometimes you make mistakes, like everybody else, and that you are going to need their help. If they hear a mistake as you read to them, they should let you know about it! Keep your tone light and amusing.

3. Give your class practice saying aloud, "What did you say?" or more simply, "What?" Tell them they must interrupt you every time you make a mistake.

4. To demonstrate, say two sentences, one correct and one ridiculous. For example, say, "Ahmed is a good student." Then say, "Ahmed is also a good mother." Everyone practices interrupting you using one of the responses in Step 3. Let them correct your mistake and thank them by saying, for example, "Oh! Right! I meant Ahmed is a good father."

5. Show students the reading. They look at it and follow along with a finger while you read aloud. Read the first sentence correctly, but in the second or third sentence make a ridiculous mistake. For example, you might say: ". . . so they got into their book and went to the store." If they are shy about saying, "What?", raise an eyebrow or repeat the mistake, saying "Their book? They got into their book?"

6. Continue to read through the story, making an occasional "mistake" and giving the students the pleasure of interrupting and correcting you. Your aim: the whole class immediately interrupts you when you make a mistake.

> This activity works equally well in an online class with no adaptations.

Extensions: In later lessons, play with phrases such as "Could you repeat that, please?", "Could you say that again?", or "Could you say that more slowly, please?"

2.8 PICTURE DICTATION

Students have such fun drawing that they may not notice how much they are learning! They use visual and spoken information to create a picture and recreate sentences. You can use this activity to review vocabulary, and it's a wonderful way to practice prepositions of location.

 AIMS: Listening for details, anchoring vocabulary by drawing, describing a picture

Procedure:

1. **Students listen:** Describe an imaginary "picture" to your class. In a low beginners' class, you might simply dictate a few nouns. With high beginners, you might review vocabulary and structures they've already studied by making up a paragraph like this:

   > In the middle of the picture there is a house. In front of the house there is a tree. Above the house there is an airplane. To the left of the house there is a new car.

2. **Students draw:** Describe the picture again, sentence by sentence, while students draw it.

3. **Students compare and talk:** In pairs, students look at their completed pictures, pointing out similarities and differences in their two drawings.

   > Online: Put a pair in each breakout room. They can hold their picture up to the camera to show their partner.

4. **A volunteer student recreates the picture on the board:** The volunteer goes to the board. The class guides them on what to draw, as necessary.

   > Online: Students return to the main room. The volunteer draws the picture on the whiteboard.

Extension: For writing practice, go to the picture on the board and point to the house. A volunteer tells you one sentence, for example, "In the middle of the picture there is a house." Write this sentence by the house. Students repeat this chorally and copy it into their own drawing. Continue until everything in the picture has a sentence by it.

2.9 GOSSIP

When students whisper a sentence to one another in a chain, it inevitably gets distorted. This activity often leads to funny results while giving students quick feedback about their pronunciation and an immediate chance to do better.

This activity works best with ten or fewer students. If you have more students, divide them into smaller groups.

 AIM: Pronouncing a sentence accurately for a classmate to repeat

Procedure:

1. Arrange students in a circle or a line. Assign one student to be Student A.

    Online: Put Student A in a breakout room.

2. Say something quietly into the ear of the first student. You can use any vocabulary or grammar you have been working with, but it should be short. For example, "I found $100 yesterday."

    Online: Join the breakout room and say the sentence to Student A.

3. This student murmurs what you said to the next person, who passes it on. (If other students can overhear as the message is passed along, teach everyone to cover their ears and hum until their turns come.)

    Online: Immediately after Step 2, add Student B to the breakout room.
        Student A tells the sentence to Student B. Return Student A to the main room and move Student C to the breakout room to be the listener.
        Student B tells the sentence they think they heard to Student C. Repeat this as students pass the sentence on to new listeners one at a time.

4. The last student tells the entire class what they heard. The results are usually hilarious.

    Online: The last students return to the main room before sharing.

5. Find out where the changes came from. In the same order, all students tell what they thought they heard. Every student will get useful feedback about their pronunciation.

6. Do another round immediately. This time, encourage everyone to speak as clearly as possible. They will!

Chapter Three

Speaking

Speaking gives us power. Too often, beginners fear that what they are saying sounds like baby talk, and too often they are spoken to as if they are children. Yet our students have mature thinking. They need to express their ideas, connect with other people, negotiate situations, and communicate their needs.

When people are learning a new language, they want to say something, and they want to say it right. These activities will help our students communicate their authentic ideas in their own voice. We can join them in the fun and the discovery.

3.1 CLASSROOM LANGUAGE

When we post helpful phrases in our classroom at the beginning of a course, students feel taken care of. They know that help is there if they need it. This is especially important for beginners, who may be living in an ongoing panic of "I don't understand" without even knowing how to tell you. Having easy access to important classroom phrases makes everyone more comfortable, which helps them learn more easily.

AIMS: Building vocabulary needed to ask for help, fostering independence in the classroom

SETUP: Make a sign with classroom phrases such as the ones below. It must be large enough to read at a distance. If you have time, make it colorful.

> Online: Post these phrases on your course site where students can easily access them.

Procedure:

1. On the first or second day with a new group, post a sign with classroom phrases in the room where everyone can see it. Include phrases like the ones below:

    *   What does _____ mean?
    *   I don't understand.
    *   How do you spell _____?
    *   How do you say _____?
    *   Can you help me, please?

    > Online: Direct students to where they can find these phrases on your course page.

2. Read each phrase aloud for the class to repeat chorally. Explain or demonstrate as needed. Tell students they can use these phrases to get help in class.

3. For the rest of your course, whenever someone struggles to say one of these phrases or says it in their native language, just smile and point to the sign.

    > Online: When necessary, share your screen to show these phrases. Students use the one they need.

4. As time goes on, encourage students to use the phrases correctly without looking at the sign. Ask the class, "Can I take this down now?" If they say, "No!" tell them, "OK, we'll take it down later."

5. When you see that they have mastered a phrase, make a celebration out of erasing that phrase, saying, "We've learned this one!"

6. From time to time, add new phrases to your sign, for example:

    *   Excuse me . . . (to get someone's attention)
    *   Could you repeat that, please?
    *   Do you have _____?
    *   Good job!
    *   Thank you!

3.2 WHAT I NEED

People love to give and receive help. Whatever you need, if you gather a group of ten people and announce your need, you will probably find help either directly from one of the ten or indirectly from someone they refer you to.

Our students usually have problems they'd like to solve, and classmates can help. This activity brings students' real concerns into the classroom. As they ask for and receive help, a climate of cohesion, friendliness, and trust develops.

 AIMS: Asking for and receiving help, practicing "want" and "need," building high-interest vocabulary around practical needs

Procedure:

1. Tell students that people can often find help if they tell a group about what they want and what they need. Students might ask for tangible items, for help with a task, or for advice. Often, classmates can help!

2. Write two sentence frames on the board. To start students thinking, you might use these examples or choose others.

   • I want a good bicycle / a conversation partner / to relax and not worry so much / help learning new words.
   • I need a driver's license / a new bed / a good night's sleep.

3. Individually, students draw or write their personal sentence completions. If they need help with vocabulary, they may turn to a classmate, a dictionary, or their teacher.

4. As students finish, put them in small groups to talk about what they wrote or drew. Encourage them to add more ideas. They may find that someone in their group can offer help.

   Online: Put a few students in each breakout room before sharing.

5. Volunteers tell the whole class what they want and what they need. Other classmates may volunteer to help. As students speak, write key words on the board. Invite choral repetition of words and sentences, for example,

   a. "Marcela needs a bicycle."
   b. "Kim has a truck."
   c. "Kim can take Marcela to a used bicycle store."

   Online: Students return to the main room.

6. As classmates offer help, give students time to make a plan or exchange phone numbers.

   Online: Students can send each other messages in the chat.

7. In a later class, volunteers tell the class how it went. You can repeat the activity, finding out about more wants and needs — and who might help.

3.3 RECONSTRUCT THE STORY

In this activity, students draw what they remember from a picture. This generates a lot of discussion about vocabulary.

 AIMS: Eliciting conversation, recalling details from a picture

MATERIALS: A picture that illustrates useful vocabulary

Procedure:

1. Pre-teach key vocabulary as needed.

2. Students look at a picture. After a short time, put the picture away.

    > Online: Share your screen to show the picture. Then stop screen sharing.

3. Students draw three things they remember from the picture.

4. As a class, they tell what they drew – a lot of information is shared because different students remembered and drew different things.

5. After the discussion, students go back to what they drew and add more things.

6. Show the original picture again. As a class, students talk about any differences between what they drew and the original picture.

    > Online: Share your screen again to show the picture.

7. Repeat the activity with another picture if students are still having fun.

Supercharge Your Teaching!

We often walk away after class wondering how it might have gone even better. "Look Back at One" is a surprisingly effective and simple way to ease our minds and improve our teaching. Try this after "Reconstruct the Story" — in fact, try using it after every class you teach! You'll find more helpful tips in our free guide *Supercharge Your Teaching*, downloadable from ProLinguaLearning.com/resources.

3.4 WHAT'S YOUR NAME? NICE TO MEET YOU!

In this activity, students mingle to practice the polite phrases they need when they meet someone new.

 AIM: Introducing oneself

Procedure:

1. On the board, write:
   A. My name is _____. What is your name?
   B. My name is _____.
   A. Nice to meet you, _____.

2. Say to your class. "My name is _____." Indicate a student and ask, "What's your name?"

3. The student responds with, for example, "My name is Sarah." (Help as needed.)

4. Go to that student and say, "Nice to meet you, Sarah." Repeat Steps 2-4 with several students until the idea is clear.

5. Point to each sentence on the board. The class repeats them chorally a few times.

6. Students copy the dialogue from the board. They mingle, talking with one classmate at a time. Encourage them to hold their paper behind their back. They may pull it out briefly if they need to see it, but they must hide it again before they speak.

> Online: Put two students in each breakout room. Shuffle the breakout rooms frequently.

7. Students continue to mingle as long as interest is high.

Note: Many teachers use name tags in the first weeks of class. They're helpful to the teacher as well as to classmates.

3.5 PLEASE AND THANK YOU

Beginners in a language need to know polite words right away. In this activity, students mingle to politely ask for items from classmates.

 AIM: Teaching *please* and *thank you*

Procedure:

1. Teach the words "book," "pen," and "paper." Write on the board:
   • Can I please have your book?
   • Can I please have your pen?
   • Can I please have your paper?
   • Thank you.

2. The class chorally repeats what's on the board several times.

3. Students stand, each holding a book, a pen, and a piece of paper.

Procedure (continued):

4. Go to a student and ask, "Can I please have your book?" while gesturing appropriately.

5. When you get the book, say, "Thank you." Repeat the procedure with a few more students. Each time, ask for something different.

6. Students stand and mingle, asking classmates for an object and saying, "Thank you." For fun, encourage them to ask for different items. Continue as long as interest is high.

> Online: Put a few students in each breakout room. After a short time, shuffle the breakout rooms.

7. Tell the class, "Please sit down." When they do, say, "Thank you!"

> Online: Students return to the main room.

Extension: If students need to return items to classmates, teach phrases like "Whose _____ is this?" and "Here's your _____, (student's name)."

3.6 READING AND SPEAKING 3 X 3

Beginners need more repetition than many of us realize. Try this activity a few times, and the whole class will be hooked! As students repeatedly read and retell the same passage, the meaning becomes clearer, and they gain a deeper unconscious understanding of how their target language functions.

AIMS:　　Improving reading comprehension, listening to retell

MATERIALS: Two reading passages (Depending on your students, these could each be a single sentence.)

Procedure:

1. Divide the class into two equal groups.

> Online: Put each half of the class in a breakout room.

2. Give every member of Group 1 a copy of something to read. They read it silently three times. Every student in Group 2 does the same with a different reading.

> Online: Post the two readings. Instruct the students to access only the reading for their group.

3. While they are reading, circulate and help as needed with vocabulary and comprehension. If students are having difficulty with some words, collect these and write them on the board.

> Online: Visit each breakout room to answer questions. Type unknown or problematic words in a document to share with the class in Step 5.

Procedure (continued):

4. After students have read their paper three times silently, they hide it and tell it from memory three times to a partner from their same group. Then that same partner will tell it to them three times. This is to prepare everyone for telling what they read to a partner who hasn't seen it yet.

> Online: Put pairs into new breakout rooms to practice. After each pair has finished practicing, they return to the main room.

5. Go over the words you've written on the board.

> Online: Share your screen to show the words.

6. Pair students. Each student will have a partner who hasn't seen the reading yet.

> Online: Create new breakout rooms. Put a pair in each room.

7. Speaking practice: Students retell their memorized passages to their new partner three times each.

8. Reading practice: Give students the passage they did not read and let them read it silently.

> Online: Ask students to read the passage that they have not yet read.

9. As a class, ask students what they remember from the reading passages.

> Online: Students return to the main room before sharing.

Note: Many of us underestimate how much repetition beginners need. If you notice that Step 9 is easy for your students, just choose longer reading passages the next time you use this activity.

 Here are two good ways to wrap up this activity: "Who Said It?" (Chapter 2, page 15) and "Add a Picture" (Chapter 4, page 36).

3.7 LET'S PUT ON A PLAY!

Here's a simple, dynamic, kinesthetic preview activity. Recreating a story as a play embeds the vocabulary and grammar of a reading deeply in students' memories.

Acting is great fun, and the reading that follows becomes a very satisfying experience. Students have so much fun that they don't even realize how much they're learning!

AIMS: Pre-teaching meaning and vocabulary, activating students with movement, role playing with new words, speaking clearly

MATERIALS: A story students can perform

Procedure:

1. Read a story to the class once or twice, clarifying words and content as needed.

2. Give students a copy of the story to follow along as you read it aloud.

> Online: Post a story where the students can access it.

3. Pair students with a partner. They read the story aloud to each other, alternating sentences. Depending on their level, students may repeat this.

> Online: Put a pair in each breakout room.

4. Now tell the class they're going to perform this story as a play. They don't need to memorize anything because they can read their parts during the play.

> Online: Students return to the main room.

5. The class decides what roles and characters are needed. If there are not enough speaking parts, use students for other parts, like a door that opens, a chair, etc. Students may volunteer, or you may assign the parts. You may need more than one narrator.

   Optional: Together with the students, make props. Often, pictures drawn on paper are good enough.

> Online: Students may make their own props that they can incorporate into their video backgrounds or foregrounds.

6. Each student writes their role or character name on a piece of paper. Students tape their signs on their chests so everyone can see who is who.

> Online: Students can temporarily change their names on their screens to that of their characters/roles.

7. Read the story aloud again as each student writes out (or mimes) what their character will say and do. Repeat this until everyone is comfortable with their parts. Students may need a lot of practice at this stage.

Procedure (continued):

8. Step back! Students perform the play. The first time is for practice; it's often such a big hilarious mess that the students are eager to perform the play two or three more times. (Optional) Invite an audience for the final performance if you can — perhaps another class, office staff, anyone walking in the hall, etc.

> Online: (Optional) Some students may want to invite a friend or family member to come and enjoy the show.

9. Talk about how the play went, what students enjoyed, and what they might change.

3.8 HOMEWORK OR QUIZ REVIEW: SEEK AND FIND

Research has shown that when we correct a set of student papers one by one and return them later, we miss an important "teachable moment." When students get immediate feedback instead — or when they identify errors and make their own corrections — they remember much more!

In this activity, students help each other correct errors in written work. This frees you for more important work and gives your students that "Aha!" moment that helps them learn.

 AIMS: Identifying errors in their own papers, learning from classmates

Procedure:

1. Read out the correct answers for a quiz or homework paper.

2. Students check their own papers, circling but not correcting items they got wrong.

3. Everyone stands and mingles, looking for papers that have correct answers to the items they got wrong.

> Online: Put a small group in each breakout room. Students tell what they got wrong and ask for help with those items.

4. When they find a classmate who does not have that word circled, they copy the correct answer on their own paper and talk about why that answer is correct.

5. Students mingle until they have found and copied all the corrections for the circles on their paper.

> Online: Shuffle the breakout rooms if necessary. Then students return to the main room when finished.

6. (Optional) They give their papers to you if you need grades — or if you want to see their errors as you plan your next lesson.

> Online: Students can submit their papers via email or post it for you on the course site.

3.9 WHAT I EAT, WHAT YOU EAT

This activity wakes students up by challenging their ability to remember new ideas as they exchange personal information with classmates. To keep it simple, choose just one verb to practice with at a time.

 AIMS: Talking about things people do every day, practicing affirmative statements, using simple present tense

Procedure:

1. Choose a common verb such as "eat."

2. Write a sentence about yourself on the board. For example, you might write "I eat apples."

3. Call on a pair of volunteers to tell each other something they like to eat. The class repeats these two sentences chorally, using their classmates' names.

4. In pairs, students tell their partner what they like to eat.

    > Online: Put a pair in each breakout room.

5. They turn to a second classmate and tell their own sentence and the one they just heard. They might say, "I eat sushi. Zeki eats hummus."

    > Online: Shuffle the breakout rooms.

6. They turn to a third classmate and tell the whole chain of information: "I eat sushi. Zeki eats hummus. Marta eats pizza." They continue with new partners, building up a chain as long as they are having fun.

    > Online: Shuffle the breakout rooms again and again.

7. As a class, volunteers tell everything they remember. Our students often amaze us!

    > Online: Students return to the main room before sharing.

Variation: On a different day, use a different verb.

Chapter Four

Reading

The minute we know how to read, we have access to street signs, forms to fill out, notes, written instructions, menus, and books. We can see the thoughts of people far away and know of places we've never been. The written world is open to us!

Reading in a new language needs a great deal of practice. The more students read, the more their vocabulary grows because they encounter their new words again and again. What may be more surprising is that reading improves all the other skills, too: listening, speaking, writing, and grammar.

The reading activities in this chapter help students read with pleasure and help us teach reading without the burden of over-preparation.

4.1 LET'S MAKE IT FALSE!

This activity helps students look closely at the details of a reading. It leads to creative thinking as they work together to make true sentences false, then gives everyone speaking practice as they quiz one another. Students sometimes come up with silly sentences, which adds to the fun!

 AIMS: Developing reading comprehension skills, practicing grammatical and syntactical control by changing details in sentences

Procedure:

1. Write on the board a sentence from a recently read passage. For example, "Mr. Jenkins has a store." Ask, "Is this true or false?" Students say, "It's true." Ask, "How can we make this false?" Volunteers offer ideas. They may change the name, the verb, or another detail. Erase and add words on the board to show these false sentences.

2. Put students in small groups and give them a copy of the reading.

> Online: Put a few students in each breakout room.

3. Students take turns reading aloud one sentence each. For every sentence, they invent one or more ways to make it false. Everyone repeats these and writes them down with help from their group. Circulate, helping if needed.

4. As a class, call on one student at a time to read one of their false sentences.

> Online: Students return to the main room before sharing.

5. Write on the board, "That's not true." If a student reads, "Mr. Jenkins has a horse," prompt the class to say chorally, "That's not true! Mr. Jenkins has a store." Continue with Steps 4 and 5 as long as students are enjoying the activity.

4.2 ON THE WALL OUTSIDE

Running and dictating in class? Why not?! In this activity, students are physically active and use all their language skills as they dictate a passage to their partner. No one gets sleepy when you use this wonderful activity! Students who read hastily often find that they forget what they just read before they reach their writing partner. This is powerful motivation for taking the time to read with full comprehension!

AIMS: Reading for full comprehension, speaking clearly, listening for information, reviewing vocabulary and grammar holistically

MATERIALS: Make a copy of a list of sentences and give it to every pair of students. For low beginners, use a picture instead.

Procedure:

1. Post several copies of the sentence list on the wall outside your classroom. Here's a typical example aimed at prepositions of place:
   - I see a table.
   - A small dog is under the table. It has a long tail.
   - A bird is over the table.
   - A big cat is on the table. The cat has a short tail.
   - A chair is next to the table. It has three legs.
   - A big picture is behind the table. It's a picture of your teacher.

   > Online: Prepare a digital version of the sentence list that you will share in Step 3.

2. Put students in pairs: a "speaker" and a "writer." Each "writer" sits at a desk with a clean piece of paper, ready to write.

   > Online: Put a pair in each breakout room. They will decide who the speaker is and who the writer is. The writer will stay in the breakout room when their speaking partner returns to the main room.

3. When you say, "Go!" each speaking partner goes outside and reads the first sentence. To make sure students use their memories for this activity, tell them not to copy or take pictures of the sentence list.

   > Online: Send a message (via chat or as a note to all the breakout rooms) that the "speaker" of each group should go to the main room. Once there, the speakers begin reading the sentence list that you will share on your screen.

4. Speakers hurry back to their partners and tell them what to write. Make sure speakers keep their hands behind their backs so that they rely on their words to do the job!

   > Online: As each speaker is ready, they return to their breakout room and dictate what they just read.

Procedure (continued):

5. When most students are about halfway through, call out, "Switch!" The partners change roles. The new speakers go back and forth until their writing partner has everything on paper. This ensures that both students can act in both roles.

6. (Optional) If some pairs finish early, they may compare their paper with what other pairs have written and discuss similarities and differences.

> Online: If some pairs finish early, they send you a message. When two groups have finished, you may put all four students in one breakout room.

7. To check their work, speakers go outside and take a picture of the sentence list. Partners take turns reading the sentences to each other as they look at their paper and make any necessary changes.

> Online: Post the sentence list so that the whole class can see it. They stay in their breakout rooms. There may be two or four students in a breakout room at this point.

Acknowledgment: This is an adaptation of an activity we learned from Kevin Keating at the University of Arizona's Center for English as a Second Language.

Supercharge Your Teaching!

As often as possible, we choose activities in which even beginners benefit from working independently. "On the Wall Outside" is one of those! You will find another, "Breathe While Students Work," in our free guide *Supercharge Your Teaching*, downloadable from ProLingualLearning.com/resources.

4.3 DICTOCOMP: REWRITING FROM KEY WORDS

Dictocomps combine Dictation and Composition. Students use all four language skills: they listen to a passage, repeat the sentences, then use key words to reconstruct the passage in writing, and finally read the original passage to check for accuracy. There's plenty of repetition in this activity, exactly what beginners need.

Dictocomps are wonderfully adaptable! Use them for pre-reading, reviewing, recycling vocabulary, or reinforcing grammar. They can also be used to teach details like punctuation and spelling.

When we use Dictocomps often, students get immediate feedback because they correct their own work. They learn more, and you don't need to correct any papers!

 AIMS: Building vocabulary to prepare for a reading, developing paraphrasing and summarizing skills, practicing accurate pronunciation

MATERIALS: A short reading passage

Procedure:

1. To pre-teach vocabulary, read your chosen passage aloud. Invite students to point out words they're not familiar with and teach these words.

2. Read the passage again one sentence at a time. Students repeat each sentence chorally. Each student chooses a word or words that will help them remember each sentence. They write these words in a list they are creating. Lower-level students may choose a few key words for each sentence; more advanced beginners often choose just one.

3. Distribute the reading. Tell students they will be using their key words to rewrite the passage. Read the passage aloud one or more times as they look at it.

   > Online: Post the reading on your course site.

4. Students hide the reading. Referring only to the key words on their list, each student writes the passage, trying to get it as close to the original as possible. Even if they don't get everything right, this is good practice!

   > Online: Make the reading unavailable.

5. Students look at the reading again and revise what they wrote, if necessary.

   > Online: Make the reading available again.

4.4 STUDENTS CHOOSE WHO'S NEXT

This read-and-repeat activity alerts students to pay very close attention to what is being read aloud because they might be called on to repeat that sentence.

 AIMS: Reading slowly for comprehension, listening closely, practicing accurate pronunciation

MATERIALS: A copy of a short reading passage for each student

Procedure:

1. Read a short passage aloud slowly, sentence by sentence. Students look at the passage and follow along with a finger.

2. Students repeat each sentence chorally so everyone has a chance to practice pronunciation. You may also call on some students individually.

3. When the passage has been read through, call on one student (Junko, for example) who stands and reads aloud the first sentence to the class.

4. Junko chooses another student. Coach her to say, for example, "Maxim, please repeat it." Junko sits down.

5. Maxim stands and repeats the sentence Junko said without looking at the text, if possible.

6. Maxim chooses a classmate to read the next sentence, saying, for example, "Maria, please read the next sentence." Maxim sits down.

7. Maria stands up. She may look at her paper to read aloud sentence number two. Then she chooses a classmate to stand up, repeat sentence number two, and read aloud sentence number three.

8. Continue until the reading is finished.

Note: Once you and your students have practiced this activity, it goes quickly.

This activity works equally well in an online class with no adaptations.

4.5 NEW WORDS AND WHAT THEY MEAN

In this lively pre-reading activity, students direct you to words they don't yet know so you can pre-teach vocabulary.

AIMS: Pre-reading to learn new words
MATERIALS: A reading passage that's new to your students
SETUP: For online classes, post the reading passage where the students can access it.

Procedure:

Pre-teach new words:

1. Give the students a reading passage. As you read it aloud, students circle words they don't know.

    > Online: Students access this reading from the course site. They can underline or highlight the words.

2. Students write these unknown words on the board. One word may appear many times; this gives you a quick survey of words you might pre-teach.

    > Online: Students put the words in the chat.

3. Choose about six of the most useful words. Pre-teach these words, keeping in mind that definitions are not the best way to approach new words. It's better to use a sketch, a synonym, a translation, an action, or a short sentence with the new word in context.

Students read the passage:

4. Students look again at the text and underline the sentences where these words appear.
5. Volunteers read aloud a sentence with one of the new words and confirm what the word means. This allows more advanced students to shine while others get an extra review.

This works very well as a demonstration before "Vocabulary Cards" (Chapter 6, page 61).

4.6 ADD A PICTURE

In this multiple intelligences activity, students recall the action in a story by drawing several sketches that show the sequence. It works very well in multilevel classes because students produce drawings rather than language.

AIMS: Recalling and telling a story, putting events in sequence

MATERIALS: A story with a series of actions (fables and simple folktales work well). Each student will need eight or nine small pieces of paper, about 4-5 inches square. They can easily tear paper to make their own pieces.

Procedure:

1. Give students a story. They follow along with a finger while you read it aloud a few times. Teach new words as needed.

   > Online: Post the story on your course site where the students can access it.

2. Students put their stories away.

   > Online: Make the story unavailable.

3. Draw on the board a very basic sketch of something that happens very early in the story. This demonstrates that they will be drawing — and that their drawings don't need to be particularly good!

4. Each student uses only three pieces of paper to start with. Tell them to draw on their first paper something they remember from the beginning of the story. Then have them draw something that happened near the end. On their third piece of paper, they draw something from the middle of the story. This will keep them from drawing only the first events in the story.

5. Each student arranges their three drawings in order on their desk with spaces between the papers. Encourage them to draw more quick sketches and put them in the spaces between their first three papers. Tell everyone they will be sharing their picture story with classmates. Continue until students have a string of pictures. (Some students will have more pictures than others, of course.)

6. As students finish, they pair up to show a partner their drawings and explain them. This works well because they will have chosen different incidents and drawn different pictures. If some pairs finish early, they may share with a new partner while they are waiting for others to finish.

   > Online: Put a pair in each breakout room. If some pairs finish early, shuffle their breakout rooms.

Extension: To add writing to this activity, some students may add captions to their pictures.

This activity would work well after "Reading and Speaking 3x3" (Chapter 3, page 24).

4.7 PREDICTING FROM THE TITLE

When we remember to give our students regular practice in predicting what they will read, their brains perk up, and they become active rather than passive readers. We can help students form this habit by looking closely at the title.

AIMS: Making and confirming predictions about a reading

MATERIALS: A short reading

Procedure:

1. Read aloud the title of the reading and write it on the board.

2. Students guess what they think this reading might be about. They dictate words for you to write or, if in person, they might draw a picture on the board.

3. Give students a copy of the reading. Read the passage aloud as they follow along with their fingers.

> Online: Share your screen to show the reading.

4. As a class, talk about how close their guesses were.

4.8 PREDICTING FROM THE PICTURE

Reading is a continual process of predicting and confirming predictions. It's far more effective to let the students guess about what they're going to read rather than telling them – and it's more fun! Pictures and other illustrations are a great prompt for predictions.

AIMS: Making and confirming predictions based on pictures in a reading

MATERIALS: A picture or illustration that goes with a reading (You may draw it yourself if there is no picture with the text.)

SETUP: For online classes, post two separate files on your course site: a picture and the reading that goes with it.

Procedure:

1. Show the picture and talk about what is in it. Tell the students that this picture goes with a reading. Ask what they think the reading might be about and write their ideas on the board.

2. Give students a copy of the reading. Read it aloud as students follow along. As you go through the reading, stop often to look at their guesses on the board. Based on students' input, mark the correct guesses with a check. Draw a line through the incorrect guesses. Put a question mark next to any guesses students aren't sure about yet.

> Online: Tell students where to access the reading on your course site.

Procedure (continued):

3. In pairs, students take turns reading the passage aloud to each other sentence by sentence.

> Online: Put a pair in each breakout room.

4. As a class, return to the guesses that have question marks. Can any of them now be marked with a check or strikethrough?

> Online: Students return to the main room to have this discussion.

4.9 TELLING BACK AND FORTH

This simple four-stage pair activity is a favorite with many teachers, and for good reason! Partners read two different short readings, then put them away. They then explain their respective readings to each other, negotiating meaning when necessary. Finally, they look back at the reading together to check the details and get immediate, personalized feedback — from the reading, not from you! This is individualized instruction at its finest, designed right into the activity! (For more information on promoting independent learning, see "Let the Activity Itself Be the Teacher" in our online resource *Supercharge Your Teaching*.)

AIMS: Re-telling and re-reading to confirm understanding, teaching information from a reading to classmates

MATERIALS: Two short readings with vocabulary students are familiar with

Procedure:

1. Tell students they will work in pairs and will each explain a short reading to their partner.

2. Put students in pairs. Give the A students one reading and the B students another reading. They read silently.

> Online: Divide your class into A's and B's. Send the A reading to all of the A's in one private message and the other reading to the B's in another message. This can be done via email or in the chat. Then put an A+B pair in each breakout room. Tell them how long they have for reading.

3. Students put their reading away when they finish reading.

> Online: Tell students to close the reading files and not look at them until they are told to do so. (This activity is neither fun nor productive if students peek.)

4. Every A student tells their B partner what they just read. "My reading says …"

Procedure (continued):

5. B repeats everything they just heard: "Oh, so your reading says__." A can repeat any information B misunderstood or forgot: "Almost right, but _____." B tells the information again until A is satisfied.

6. A and B look at A's reading together to discover whether B's retelling was complete and correct. Direct them by saying, "Four eyes on one paper." Students are eager to see what they got right, and if they discover mistakes, they get immediate feedback.

> Online: A shares their screen to look at the reading with B.

7. When most pairs are finished with A's reading, they switch roles. Now it is B's turn to teach what they read using steps 4-6. Give B students a moment to review their reading and then have them put it away again.

> Online: In the chat, send a message to all the breakout rooms telling students to switch roles. Tell the B students they can look at their reading again. Give them a short time to review it before repeating steps 4-6.

Chapter Five

Writing

Writing lets us communicate across space and time. We write to fill out a job application. We write to leave a note for a friend. Even the act of writing our own name can be a step into empowerment in a new language. Eventually, we write to organize, even to discover, our own ideas. We write to express ourselves. Writing is the most challenging of the language skills for students, and it can be the most time-consuming work a teacher does. This chapter aims to help!

5.1 LET'S LEARN THOSE LETTERS

This activity uses action and plenty of repetition to help students who are learning a new alphabet.

 AIMS: Teaching alphabet letters

Procedure:

1.   Teach the letters a few at a time. Write each one on the board as you say its name and make a sound this letter frequently represents. Students repeat each letter chorally and then individually.

2.   Students "write" each letter in the air as they name the letter and make the sound.

3.   Students stand in a long line and trace each letter several times on the back of a classmate as you say the letter and make the sound. You may wish to specify lowercase or capital letters since some students will probably ask about that.

> Online: Students use a finger to "write" the letter on their other hand, then their leg, other parts of their body, and their desk.

4.   After introducing a few letters, start pointing on the board to letters you've taught in previous lessons, inviting students to call out the name of each letter. If students succeed in recalling the letters you've already practiced, introduce a few more.

Extension: Just for fun, you might put students in pairs and have them take turns writing letters on each other's backs, except that only the student who is drawing the letters knows which letter is being drawn. The student whose back is being written on tries to guess the letters.

> Online: Put pairs in breakout rooms. Have students write the letters in the air with their fingers.

 This activity can be followed by "Alphabet on the Wall: Collecting Words" (Chapter 6, page 65).

5.2 FILL-IN-THE-BLANK DICTATION

Unstressed words in speech are often misused or even left out in students' writing. With fill-in-the-blank activities, students teach themselves where these words belong in grammatically correct sentences. In this activity, students create unique fill-in-the-blank passages, then exchange them and try to reconstruct the sentences. They get to correct their work immediately, which makes learning more memorable. Because students will be copying model sentences, this activity is good for your low beginners.

AIMS: Developing grammatical and word-order awareness, recalling details from a reading

MATERIALS: A reading passage

SETUP: For online classes, post a reading passage on your course site.

Procedure:

Getting Ready

1. Hand out a reading passage and read it to your students.

> Online: Tell students where to access the reading on your course site.

2. Individually, students copy the reading. In each sentence, they leave out one word every four to seven words and put a blank space there instead. Different students will leave out different words. For example:

    • "Alex____ only 12 years old, but ____ helps everyone in his ____ with English."

    • "Alex is ____ 12 years old, ____ he helps everyone in ____ family with English."

> Online: Students type their fill-in-the-blank version in a document to share with a partner in Step 4.

Note: Why do we ask them to create their own papers? This step saves us preparation time and gives our students some useful copying practice.

Filling in the Blanks: The Dictation

3. Students put away the original reading passage.

> Online: Make the passage unavailable.

4. In pairs, students exchange the papers they created. Individually, students fill in the blanks in their partner's paper, looking only at this paper.

> Online: Put a pair in each breakout room. Students share their fill-in-the-blank documents with their partners via email or another convenient way.

5. When students have completed each other's exercises, they check their answers with each other.

Procedure (continued):

6. Students may look back at the original passage if needed.

> Online: Make the passage available again.

Acknowledgment: This is a zero-preparation variation of an activity we learned in a workshop from Mario Rinvolucri.

5.3 LET'S FIND SOME USEFUL MISTAKES!

Want to save yourself a huge amount of time marking written work — and empower your students to make new mistakes, not old ones? In this activity, you choose some sentences with typical errors. The class offers ideas about how to correct them, and every student gets a chance to edit their own written work.

 AIMS: Correcting common errors as a group, demonstrating the value of editing one's own writing

Procedure:

1. Assign a piece of in-class writing. While students are writing, circulate to collect some sentences with common errors.

> Online: Use an application or program that will allow you to see students' writing instantly.

2. When students are finished, write on the board one of the sentences you collected, such as "I love my dress red." Don't mention who wrote it.

3. Ask students how this sentence might be corrected and write on the board the changes they offer. If a suggestion is not correct, write it on the board anyway as a springboard for discussion and further corrections.

4. Give students time to look for and correct similar errors in their own papers.

5. Repeat Steps 3-4 with the other sentences you collected.

6. You may end the activity here, or collect the papers if you need grades. You'll have fewer "old" errors to mark, leaving you more time and energy to correct "new" errors.

 This activity works well after "Partners in Writing" (Activity 5.7).

Supercharge Your Teaching!

Students are often quiet because they're nervous about making mistakes, but whether you call it the "zone of proximal development" or "interlanguage" or "the edge of learning," mistakes are where language learning happens! To put students at ease and encourage them, see "That's a Great Mistake!" in our free guide *Supercharge Your Teaching*, downloadable from ProLinguaLearning.com/resources.

5.4 CHAIN STORY

Because the class is making up their own story, interest is high! The example given here lets students practice past tense grammar. You can guide the story toward practicing other forms, or you can let the students' collective imagination take all of you for a wild ride.

 AIMS: Building confidence in writing, practicing verb tenses

Procedure:

1. Dictate the first sentence of a story to students. For example: "We went to Africa."

2. One at a time, students add a sentence in the past tense. Each student must repeat the previous sentence before adding their own, for example, "We went to Africa. We walked to the desert." Students write down the sentences they hear as the activity continues.

   One class created this story: "We went to Africa. We walked to the desert. We were hot. We drank water. Many animals ran to the jeep. Peng killed a lion."

   Here are three good ways to do this. Choose the one that's best for your class.

   a. For low beginners, as you hear each sentence, write it on the board for everyone to copy. Make the needed corrections as you go.

   b. Here's a more student-centered option: Two or more students at the board write what they hear the speakers say. The class offers suggestions for corrections if needed; then everyone adds the sentence to their growing list.

   > Online: The teacher writes the sentences.

   c. For more advanced beginners, each student writes what they hear the speakers say. They may look at two classmates' papers to see whether they've written the same thing.

   > Online: Put a small group in each breakout room. They take turns sharing their screen to look at each other's papers.

4. Each student writes a few more sentences to extend the story in their own way. One student wrote, "We made a B.B.Q. We ate the lion. We went home."

5. In small groups, students read their entire stories to one another.

   > Online: Put a small group in each breakout room if you chose option A or B above.

6. Each group chooses one story to read aloud to the whole class.

   > Online: Students return to the main room before sharing.

7. (Optional) Post all stories for everyone to read and enjoy.

5.5 THE APPEARING AND DISAPPEARING SENTENCE

This fun writing and re-writing activity is excellent for low beginners because it provides plenty of repetition.

 AIMS: Strengthening sight-sound recognition, practicing spelling

Procedure:

1. Write a sentence on the board and read it aloud.

    Online: Share your screen to show the sentence.

2. Students repeat the sentence chorally, in groups, and perhaps individually.

3. Erase one of the words.

4. Individually, students write the sentence, restoring the missing word.

5. The class calls out the missing word, and you or a volunteer student rewrites it in the sentence on the board.

6. The class chorally repeats the sentence.

7. Erase two or more words from the same sentence. As before, students repeat the full sentence, then write the full sentence, restoring what you erased. Call out those words while you or a volunteer restores them. Then the class chorally repeats the sentence.

8. Repeat the activity, increasing the challenge by first erasing whole phrases and then the entire sentence.

5.6 THE VOCABULARY OF SENTENCES AND PARAGRAPHS

This activity gives students a model of what sentences and paragraphs should look like. It also serves as a handy reference for labels you'll be using often in a writing class. Because they create the model page themselves, students learn more than they would if you gave it to them as a handout. Tell them to keep it in their notebooks or folders so they can refer to it as they write and before handing in written work. There's plenty of repetition here, so it's suitable for beginners.

 AIMS: Learning vocabulary about the conventions of writing sentences and paragraphs

MATERIALS: A copy for each student of a short paragraph to demonstrate the features a paragraph should include. Online students will need to copy this on paper themselves in order to add the symbols.

Procedure:

1. Give students a simple paragraph without labels, reading it aloud to them. You can easily create a different paragraph to interest your students.

Procedure (continued):

About Our Class

Jan Herron is my writing teacher. We didn't come to class on Monday because it was a holiday. Classes started on Tuesday. Jan's class is fun! Today we did a dictation, and I think dictations are a good way to learn. What is your favorite class activity?

> Online: Share your screen to show the paragraph. Students copy this on their own paper.

2. Ask, "Where is the title?" Volunteer students tell you where it is. If they don't know, point it out yourself. Write "title" off to the side, with an arrow pointing to "About Our Class." Students add "title" and the arrow to their papers as shown in the illustration below.

3. In the same way, elicit or teach the following labels

   - paragraph
   - first line
   - indent
   - capital letter
   - comma
   - period
   - apostrophe
   - question mark
   - exclamation point

When you are finished, your students' paragraph will look like this:

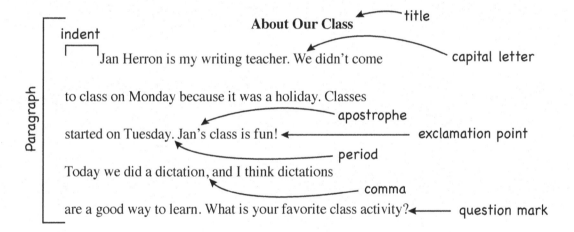

4. To practice the labels orally, point to each feature of the paragraph. Say, for example, "Indent here." Students repeat chorally, "Indent here." Continue pointing to each feature and naming it so students can repeat it chorally.

5. Go through the labeled features again. This time, say, "What is this?" as you point to each one. The class tells you what it is.

6. To reinforce the new vocabulary the next time students write sentences or paragraphs, invite them to look at the model they created. Ask the class questions like "Did you indent?", "Did you remember the title?", "Did you start every sentence with a capital letter?", "Did you use periods, commas, and other punctuation correctly?" For each element they did correctly, encourage them to raise their hands and call out, "Yes, I did!" The satisfaction of success is fun, and you will have fewer errors to mark if you collect their papers.

5.7 PARTNERS IN WRITING

Students, especially beginners, often speak more naturally than they write in their target language. This may be because in writing there is more time to compose a thought in the first language, translate it mentally, then write it down — which often carries with it some interlanguage errors.

In this activity, students speak to a partner first, then immediately write. The result is more-natural language. Students also have a real audience for what they're writing. Their partner may understand (or not understand) and may be interested (or not). All of this is useful information for a writer! It helps student writers catch errors as they commit words to paper.

 AIMS: Writing a paragraph on a topic, speaking and listening to classmates

Procedure:

Getting ready to write:

1. Talk briefly about a topic your students can write about. Instead of saying, for example, "We're going to write about our families," launch right into a story of your own to capture their attention. For example, "I remember my grandmother. Her kitchen smelled wonderful! She gave me cookies after school."

2. Tell students they will talk about their families with a partner. To demonstrate what pairs will do, bring one student up to the board as your partner. Say, "I remember my grandmother." Write this on the board as your partner watches. Then switch roles: coach the student to say a short sentence about their family and help them write it on the board.

> Online: Ask the student volunteer to write the sentence in the chat.

Partner writing:

3. In pairs, students tell their partners a few sentences about the topic. After each sentence, the student who spoke writes it down. Their listening partners look on, helping the writer if necessary. Announce when it's time to switch roles.

> Online: Put a pair in each breakout room. The speaking partner shares their screen.

4. Students reread their whole paragraph to their partner.

5. Students may mingle, reading their paragraph to one classmate after another.

> Online: Shuffle the breakout rooms.

 This activity works well before "Let's Find Some Useful Mistakes!" (Activity 5.3).

5.8 EDITING AND REVISION: I CAN DO IT MYSELF

This routine saves the composition teacher a great deal of time by strengthening students' internal correctness "monitors." Throughout your course, each student keeps a growing list of what they know they can do correctly. Before they hand in a new piece of writing, students refer to their list and correct any "old" errors that crept in. Students feel empowered, and the teacher is free to concentrate on helping with new errors.

AIMS: Building confidence in writing, practicing verb tenses

MATERIALS: A stapler and a simple two-pocket folder for each student (This will hold formal compositions but no other work.)

> Online: Create a digital composition folder for each student. Use an application such as Google Docs or Microsoft Teams that will allow you to see changes instantly.

Procedure:

1. Each student writes their name on the outside of their folder.

2. Write on the board these two sentences:
   - "I can always do these things correctly."
   - "I checked these things, and I am ready to give my composition to my teacher."

3. Each student writes the first sentence at the top of a clean piece of paper and the second sentence at the bottom. They staple this paper on the left inside of their folder.

> Online: Students will type these two sentences in an online document entitled "Things I Can Do Correctly."

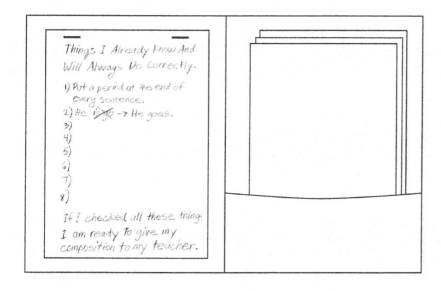

Procedure (continued):

4. Ask students what they can do correctly in their compositions. To help them get started, write on the board such ideas as:

   - "I put a title in the center of the first line."

   - "I begin each sentence with a capital letter."

   - "I end each sentence with a period."

   - "I indent the first line of a paragraph."

   > Online: View the students' compositions online while they are working. If appropriate, tell students to look at items in their list.

5. Students start their personal list by writing the number "1" on their paper. They copy from the list on the board something they know they can always do correctly and add an example. They continue listing more things, with each student including only what they are confident they will never do incorrectly in a paper they hand in.

   This paper remains in their folder throughout your course, along with successive drafts of compositions in the pocket on the right. Each time you teach a writing lesson, ask whether anyone wants to add a skill to their list. It is important that students, not you, choose what goes on their lists.

   > Online: Students should save their document in their online folder.

6. Before students hand in each composition, give them class time to edit it while referring to their list. Encourage them to look for only one error at a time. This will take some modeling and persistence until students notice for themselves how many errors they miss when they don't take time to check their work carefully.

   While this is going on, circulate. If you see an error that a student has claimed mastery of, just point to their list, not the composition. They should be able to find that error on their own.

7. If you have collected their work, you have each student's list in front of you, stapled into their folder. It takes very little time to scan it before reading the composition. If you do find an error that a student has claimed mastery of, you have options:

   a. If a student is usually conscientious but somehow missed one error, you might write in the margin the number of that error from their list with a friendly question mark.

   b. You can simply stop reading and return that paper to the student.

   c. You may automatically adjust the grade.

   You are projecting confidence. Students rise to our expectations and take charge of their own learning.

 This can be done after "The Vocabulary of Sentences and Paragraphs" (Activity 5.6).

5.9 SPELLING IMPROVEMENT

In this activity, students spell vocabulary words as you dictate them. The steps that follow give beginning students the repetition they need.

AIM: Practicing spelling of previously taught vocabulary
MATERIALS: A list of 5-10 spelling words you want students to practice

Procedure:

1. Dictate each vocabulary word you have chosen, making sure students understand the meanings. Students write the words to practice spelling them.

2. A volunteer goes to the board. To practice saying the alphabet letters, the class calls out how the volunteer should spell each word. Students self-correct their own papers as words go up on the board.

> Online: The volunteer shares their screen to show how they are spelling the word.

3. When the list on the board is complete, the class says each word chorally, then the spelling, and then the word again.

5.10 ONE-MINUTE FEEDBACK

Why wait for the end of the course to find out from our students what they are learning? Here's a quick activity many teachers use frequently. When students write a note at the end of class about one thing they learned, they benefit in at least two ways. First, when they know at the beginning of class that they'll be asked for a feedback note at the end, they pay more attention during the lesson to what they understand and don't understand and ask more questions during class. Second, when students look back at the lesson to write their note at the end of class, they remember more!

The teacher benefits too: a quick review of their notes after class lets you know what you need to clarify or re-teach next time. Best of all, you get to see what your students did learn. This feels like a pat on the back, something we get too little of!

AIMS: Reviewing a lesson, writing or drawing a short note about something they learned.
SETUP: For online classes, create an online form for each student.

Procedure:

1. When students come into class, ask them to set aside a small piece of paper on which they will write (at the end of class) something they learned.

2. Near the end of class, give students time to glance back at the lesson, choose something they learned, draw or write it on their blank note, and give it to you as they leave. They don't need to sign these notes.

> Online: Share the link to the online form for students to write their note.

3. Glance through these notes after class. They will warm your heart, and they often help with planning your next lesson.

Chapter Six

Vocabulary

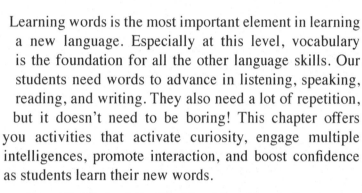

Learning words is the most important element in learning a new language. Especially at this level, vocabulary is the foundation for all the other language skills. Our students need words to advance in listening, speaking, reading, and writing. They also need a lot of repetition, but it doesn't need to be boring! This chapter offers you activities that activate curiosity, engage multiple intelligences, promote interaction, and boost confidence as students learn their new words.

Three Essential Principles for Teaching Vocabulary

1. What are the three stages of learning a new word?

All students go through the same process with a new word: first it's a stranger, then they befriend it, then they get to know it well. That's why we have organized these activities into three stages:

- Stage 1 - Meet the Words: initial exposure to new words

- Stage 2 - Work with the Words: manipulating and recycling them

- Stage 3 - Make the Words My Own: deeper understanding and long-term retention

Many of us unconsciously gravitate toward activities at Stage 1, 2, or 3. Once we're aware of this, we can expand our repertoire, making sure we are providing instruction in all three stages of vocabulary learning. This chapter helps you do just that!

2. How many words can students learn?

A general guideline is to focus on no more than 5 to 8 words per lesson. However, every student is different! Throughout a course, we can individualize by giving eager students a say in how many words they intend to learn.

3. How frequently should students review words?

Spaced learning, with increasing time between reviews, is much more powerful than intensively studying a word. For example, coach students to use their vocabulary cards (page 61) to review their new words after 5 minutes / 30 minutes / a few hours / the end of the day / 24 hours / one week / one month.

53

STAGE 1 - MEET THE WORDS

Introducing Total Physical Response: Learning Through Movement

Is TPR the most useful strategy in our repertoire for beginning students? Many teachers think so! James Asher's Total Physical Response Method is based on acting out words or sentences. It provides holistic learning of vocabulary, grammar, and pronunciation, and it bridges students to speaking, reading, and writing.

With TPR, students learn language very much the same way young children learn their first language. Students need to understand before they can speak, and TPR lets them learn language by moving their bodies before they actually say the words. This multisensory experience has a powerful effect on recall, so it boosts fluency and confidence!

TPR is ideal in multi-level classes because each student performs at their own level, glancing at their classmates' actions for support as needed. And many teachers find it essential for beginning learners when the teacher isn't familiar with the native language (L1) of the students; no translation is needed because the actions make the meaning clear.

Why use TPR?

- It's fun! Students feel like they are playing games, so motivation and attention are high.
- It reduces anxiety, which is especially important for beginners.
- The best reason to use TPR is that the physical actions "anchor" meaning so students remember much more than with other teaching methods.

6.1 CLASSIC TOTAL PHYSICAL RESPONSE (TPR): ACTIONS TELL THE STORY

The classic 5-step version of TPR is an indispensable routine for teachers of beginners.

AIMS: Learning vocabulary by listening to directions and acting them out, saying steps in a sequence

MATERIALS: A set of actions in a sequence. You can find many TPR sequences online or create your own. Here is an example. For online classes, post this on your course site.

Example TPR Sequence: Getting Ready for School

- Wake up.
- Get out of bed.
- Put on your clothes.
- Eat breakfast.

- Brush your teeth.
- Get your books.
- Go out.
- Lock your door.
- Go back! Get your cell phone.
- Go out again.
- Lock your door again.
- Walk to school.
- Say, "Good morning, everyone!"

Procedure:

1. Students just observe: For each line, you speak and do the actions while students watch and listen.

2. Students add actions: You speak and do the actions again while students do the actions silently.

> Online: Students complete all of the actions with their cameras on.

3. Students add speaking: You speak but DO NOT act. Students repeat and do the actions.

4. Give students a copy of the sentences. Choose a student and demonstrate what pairs will do. First, you say the sequence while the student does the actions. Then switch.

> Online: Post the sentences in the chat or on your course site.

5. Students work on their own: Pair students to practice in the same way. This is where most of the practice happens. Students should do it several times, with the same or different partners. Let students decide how much is enough.

> Online: Put a pair in each breakout room. Feel free to shuffle the breakout rooms.

Tips for Success:

- Each step should be repeated several times, until most students are doing it correctly without looking to see what classmates are doing.

- Make sure that your actions show the meaning very clearly. Also, be sure that every student imitates your actions. Without this physical activity, the words won't mean much or stay in their memories.

- Some students may begin speaking while they do the actions as early as Step 2. Others won't speak so soon. This is OK. They are all learning by doing the actions.

6.2 TPR: MAKING A PEANUT BUTTER SANDWICH

This variation of TPR adds some writing. The peanut butter sandwich is a classic American food. Students can even make and eat their own sandwiches during class.

AIMS: Listening to directions and acting them out, saying steps in a sequence, copying sentences

MATERIALS: A jar of peanut butter, two slices of bread, and a knife. You might bring enough peanut butter and bread for the whole class. Find out in advance if some students are allergic to nuts. If you or any students are allergic, choose a different food.

Procedure:

1. Tell the class, "I love peanut butter sandwiches." Hold up the jar and say, "peanut butter."

2. Make yourself a sandwich, take a bite and say, "Mmm. . . good." Students may wonder why you are doing this in a language classroom.

3. Ask, "How do we make a peanut butter sandwich?" Tell the steps, acting them out as you go. Students watch and listen silently.

The sequence:

- Open the peanut butter jar.

- Get two slices of bread.

- Get some peanut butter from the jar.

- Spread the peanut butter on one slice of bread.

- Put the other slice on top.

- Sit down and eat your sandwich. Say, "What a good sandwich! I love peanut butter."

4. Act and say the sequence a few more times. Students act but do NOT speak. They will look at classmates if they forget what a word means.

5. Say the sequence but do not act it out. Students do the actions and speak as much as they can. Repeat, moving on only when the students are speaking with confidence.

6. Students copy the sequence as you write it on the board.

7. In pairs, students take turns using the sequence. One reads, and the listening partner (who cannot see the paper) repeats and acts. Then they switch roles.

> Online: Put a pair in each breakout room.

8. Invite students to make vocabulary cards for words they want to remember from this activity.

> Online: Students return to the main room.

 This activity works well with "Vocabulary Cards" (Activity 6.7).

6.3 TPR: WORKING WITH MONEY

This interactive activity uses physical manipulation of objects to teach the vocabulary of money and numbers. It can get pretty silly!

AIMS: Learning the names of coins and bills, practicing cardinal numbers

MATERIALS: A quarter, a dime, a nickel, a penny, (or the coinage your students need to learn), and various bills of different values

Procedure:

Whole-Class Practice

1. Pre-teach vocabulary by holding up each coin and bill. Say its name and write it on the board. The whole class repeats each one several times.

> Online: Share your screen to show pictures of the different coins and bills.

2. Call on students one at a time to say the words as you point to them.

3. Hand out one coin or bill to each of several students.

> Online: Give students a few minutes to find some coins and bills (or, even better, ask students prior to the class to be prepared with them).

4. Now the fun begins! Ask a student to give their money to another student, for example: "Petra, please give your dollar to Anima."

> Online: Ask students one at a time to hold up a coin or bill to the camera, giving a classmate the money virtually.

5. Repeat Step 4 until students know the names of these coins and bills well.

6. Add to the task by asking students to give directions to classmates about what to do with the money they're holding. Encourage students to use items that other classmates haven't used yet. For example, Saad says, "Maria, please give the dollar to Sachiko." Or Saad may say, "Maria, please put the ten-dollar bill in your bag." Students get creative; this step generates a lot of laughter.

> Online: Ask students one at a time to hold up a coin or bill to the camera and tell a classmate what to do with it. The classmate will mime this action.

Pair Practice

7. Demonstrate by telling students, "I want to buy a pair of shoes for $26.67. What coins and bills will I need?" Elicit an answer: "A twenty-dollar bill, a five-dollar bill, a one-dollar bill, two quarters, a dime, a nickel, and two pennies." Then elicit a different set of coins and bills that will add up to $26.67.

Procedure (continued):

8. Put students in pairs. Student A names something to buy and what it might cost. Student B writes it down and tells a way to pay cash for this. They switch roles and continue until you end the activity.

> Online: Put a pair in each breakout room.

9. Volunteers may tell one example from their pair work.

> Online: Students return to the main room before sharing.

Variation: Try this sometimes with school supplies or other sets of objects.

6.4 FROM PICTURES TO WORDS

This activity is a powerful way to learn new words. Each student brings a picture of an object or action they recently decided to learn the name of. Then they teach their new word to the whole class.

AIMS: Practicing words students have chosen to learn, practicing the question, "What is that?"

SETUP: Each student brings a picture of an object or action they recently learned the name of.

Procedure:

1. Invite students to take out the picture they brought.
2. Write on the board, "What is that?" Practice this with your class using choral repetition.
3. One at a time, students show their picture to the class.

> Online: Students share their screen to show their picture.

4. As a class, students chorally ask, "What is that?"
5. The student answers, for example, "a paper bag" or "running." The class repeats this.
6. Continue until everyone has had a turn.
7. To review the vocabulary, some students show their picture again as the class chorally calls out the word. They may make vocabulary cards for the most useful words (see page 61).

6.5 PRACTICING COUNTING

Numbers are so deeply ingrained in our minds that many people still count in their native language long after they are fluent in their target language. This game gives students the opportunity to practice saying numbers in a fun and lively way.

 AIM: Practicing numbers and counting

MATERIALS: (Optional) A few objects to use as prizes

Procedure:

1. Give students a moment to find three small objects that can be hidden in one hand. Small pieces of paper work fine.

2. (Optional) Put a few small prizes where everyone can see them.

> Online: This is not needed in an online class.

3. Each student takes their three objects and secretly hides zero, one, two, or three of them in one hand. They put this hand with the object(s) on top of their desk.

4. Individually, each student calls out their guess about the cumulative total for the whole class. In a class of ten, for example, the highest possible number is thirty. Students must pronounce numbers clearly so they all can understand everyone's guess.

5. After all guesses are spoken, call on students around the class. Each student holds up zero, one, two, or three fingers to show how many objects they're holding in their other hand. Chorally, the class counts the total number of objects until the count reaches the total for the whole class.

6. Congratulate the student who had the closest guess or (optional) award them a prize.

> Online: Announce the name of the winning student, and classmates use the "clap hands" icon to reward them.

7. If interest is high, play more than one round of this game.

    Variation: For large classes, play in small groups with more objects in each student's hand.

> Online: Put a small group in each breakout room.

6.6 GETTING TO KNOW YOU: A BIRTHDAY GAME

This activity provides plenty of repetition of calendar-related vocabulary as students get acquainted and gather information about one another.

 AIMS: Practicing months of the year, ordinal numbers, possessive pronouns, and students' names

Procedure:

1. Show the class a list of all the months and the first five ordinal numbers ("first, second, third, fourth, fifth").

2. Recite the months and the ordinal numbers. The class repeats them chorally after you. You will teach other ordinal numbers as the activity goes along.

3. As you silently point to each word, the class says it chorally. Repeat this until your students can say the words without your modeling them.

4. Choose a student and ask, "What is your name?". The student responds, "My name is _____." (for example, Isslemou) Write his name on the board.

5. Ask, "Isslemou, when is your birthday?" Help him form the complete sentence, "My birthday is February 10th."

6. Ask, "What is his name?" Coach the class to respond chorally with a complete sentence to practice possessive pronouns: "His name is Isslemou." Make sure everyone is speaking.

7. Ask the class, "When is Isslemou's birthday?" The class answers chorally, "His birthday is February 10th." Some students may need a little more listening before they speak, so repeat this step until every student is speaking.

8. Isslemou chooses a classmate. Repeat steps 4-7. For each student, write their name and birthday on the board.

9. To review and for more practice, point to one name at a time on the board. Coach the class to chorally say for each name on the board, "____'s birthday is ____."

Note: If someone has a birthday during your course, you might plan a party!

This activity works equally well in an online class with no adaptations.

6.7 VOCABULARY CARDS

Ask students what they need, and most will give you the same answer: more words. They are right! This activity helps students remember the words they are learning as your course goes along. Vocabulary Cards work better than writing lists in a notebook or an online document because

- They can post cards on their refrigerator, their bathroom mirror, etc.
- They can easily remove cards once they've mastered a word, keeping only the words they need to continue reviewing.
- They can quiz themselves by using the cards as flashcards.
- They can play games with the cards and re-arrange them, in class and at home.

AIMS: Reviewing vocabulary repeatedly for deep learning

MATERIALS: Enough index cards to give each student three or four. Later, they can buy their own cards. If this is not possible where you teach, students may cut pieces of paper into cards of about 3 to 5 inches each.

Procedure:

How to create vocabulary cards:

1. Every time students want to remember a word they just learned, they make a vocabulary card. On the front, the student prints the new word as large as possible.

2. On the back, the student writes a translation or makes a quick sketch. Every card must also have a short sentence in the target language using the new word in context. This sentence can come from the teacher or from the student's own experiences. Note: It's best to start with translations or sketches because definitions are notoriously hard to understand and remember.

3. As they get to know a word better over time, students may add similar words or opposites, notes about pronunciation or part of speech, etc.

Three ways to use vocabulary cards:

A. Students quiz themselves: Students use these as flashcards in class and at home by looking at the front and trying to remember the word, then using it in a sentence. If they need help, they can look on the back.

B. Students quiz each other: In class, pairs play a game in which each partner holds several of their vocabulary cards in one hand like a fan. They can see only the words on the front, and their partner sees only the backs. One student at a time chooses a random card in their partner's hand. The card holder uses that word in a sentence. If they are successful, they lay that card down. If they needed help, they look at the back, then return that card to the collection in their hand. They continue taking turns quizzing each other as long as interest is high.

> Online: Put a pair in each breakout room. Students hold their cards up to the camera.

Procedure (continued):

C. Students categorize their cards: Students take out all their cards and arrange them into categories. Then they tell a classmate why they sorted them in this way. Typical categories might be parts of speech, words I know well or words I need to review more often, colors, furniture, parts of the body, or clothing. Categorizing is a great way to anchor words in memory. Students often come up with their own categories.

> Online: Put a pair in each breakout room. Students hold up one category of cards at a time to the camera.

6.8 HALF A PICTURE

In this activity, students predict what they will see in the missing second half of a picture. They are generating vocabulary about the visible half and brainstorming ideas about the whole picture. The whole class does this together, so if a student knows few or no words about the picture, that's okay. Curiosity makes them eager to see the second half, so interest is high! This makes the words more memorable.

AIMS: Making predictions, generating and collecting useful words
MATERIALS: An interesting picture with high-frequency vocabulary

Procedure:

1. Hold up the picture with the right-hand half of it hidden.

> Online: Use a snipping tool to divide the picture in half. Share your screen to show half of the picture.

2. With the whole class, talk about the half of the picture that's visible. Write some of these words on the board.

3. Ask about the missing second half by saying, "I wonder what's in the other half."

4. As the class calls out predictions about what might be there, write their ideas on the board. Ask questions if they need prompting.

5. Reveal the whole picture with enthusiasm.

> Online: Share your screen with the whole picture.

6. Erase from the board predictions that turned out not to be in the picture. Talk about the guesses that were correct and add new vocabulary that students didn't think of before.

7. Students make vocabulary cards with words they want to remember.

See "Vocabulary Cards" (Activity 6.7).

6.9 ALL THE WORDS WE KNOW

Here's a way to boost the confidence of your students early in your course. Many students feel intimidated by the new language and are sure that everyone knows more than they do. This activity shows them how many words they already know. Beginners are often surprised and delighted!

 AIMS: Helping students discover how many words they already know, learning new words from classmates

Procedure:

1. Say, "We are going to learn many new words, but you already know a lot of words, like phone, computer, dollar, and okay." Write these on the board.

2. In small groups, students make a list of all the words they already know in the target language. They can make sketches if they can name a word but don't know how to write it.

> Online: Put a small group in each breakout room.

3. As a class, to get a full list without duplicates, a volunteer from one group reads out their list. Write each word on the board. If students in the other groups have the same word, they cross it off their list.

> Online: Students return to the main room before sharing.

4. The next group reads out their remaining words. Continue until you have a list of unduplicated words on the board.

5. Name the words out loud. Students chorally repeat the words.

6. (Optional) Invite volunteers to name any words they aren't sure about. Teach the meanings of these words.

6.10 MANIPULATING OBJECTS OR PICTURES

The three TPR activities in Stage One, "Classic Total Physical Response (TPR): Actions Tell the Story," "TPR: Making A Peanut Butter Sandwich," and "TPR: Working with Money" use the full 5-step TPR method to move students into independent pair work for full mastery.

This activity has elements of TPR because they can look at what classmates are doing to make sure they understood you correctly, and they manipulate real objects to activate their kinesthetic intelligence. Deep learning while having fun — what could be better?

AIMS: Practicing vocabulary with real objects or pictures of objects, working with prepositions of place

SETUP: Every student will need the same set of 5-6 objects. You can supply the objects (or pictures), or your students can. To save time in an online class, have students collect their objects ahead of time.

Procedure:

1. Tell students what objects everyone should put on their desk.

2. Start giving directions about how to move them around. Students chorally repeat your words as they do each action.

> Online: If necessary, give students a few minutes to find common items you name and bring them to their computer.

Here is one possible set of instructions:

- Pick up the book.

- Put down the book.

- Pick up the pencil.

- Put down the pencil.

  Note: Continue using "pick up" and "put down" if you need to teach the names of some other objects before students start manipulating them.

- Put the pencil beside the book.

- Put the book on the pencil.

- Put the pencil in the book.

- Put your cell phone under your chair.

- Give the pen to a classmate.

3. (Optional) Volunteer students call out instructions for the class to do.

6.11 ALPHABET ON THE WALL: COLLECTING WORDS

If you have the same classroom every day with wall space available for your own use, here's a good activity for students learning a new alphabet. You gain an ongoing display of the alphabet in your room, with a growing collection of words your students are learning. You'll refer to this display again and again.

AIM: Recognizing letters and the sounds they typically represent
MATERIALS: Pieces of paper, tape

Procedure:

1. Post each alphabet letter on the wall around the room, in both capital and lower case.

   > Online: Create a document for each letter and post the documents in a folder on the discussion board.

2. Each student writes their name on a piece of paper and posts it under the letter it starts with.

   > Online: Students can post this on the discussion board.

3. As you introduce new words throughout your course, students write each word in the wall dictionary. Here's an example of how it might look.

Aa	Bb	Cc	Dd	Ee
Alfredo	Blanca	Carmen	Daud	Ernesto
apple	boy	circle	dog	elephant
are	bread	cat	daddy	eat

4. Periodically, ask students to read out loud the words written under each letter. Doing this gives students a good review of the sounds each letter can represent.

Extension: You can find creative ways to review the words on your wall. For example, students can make up sentences using the words, or see how many words they can use in a story.

6.12 TWO UNRELATED PICTURES: HOW ARE THEY THE SAME?

It is always a mental adventure to find similarities in things that looked very different at first glance. Even beginners can experience this "Aha!" when you use pictures to generate vocabulary. In this activity, each student gets to explore their own "memory bank" of words. They are often surprised at how many words their group knows in the target language!

AIM: Generating vocabulary from pictures
MATERIALS: Several pictures of objects

Procedure:

1. Choose two unrelated pictures, for example, a hammer and a chair. Hold them up and ask the class, "How are these the same?"

    > Online: Share your screen to show the two pictures.

2. Volunteers answer. Help them formulate one or two sentences such as "They are brown. They are in a house." Write these on the board and circle the key words, for example, "brown" and "in a house".

3. In small groups, students look at the circled words. They make lists of other things that share each characteristic. For example, they might list things that are brown and things one might find in a house.

    > Online: Put a small group in each breakout room after the students copy the circled words.

4. As a class, groups report some of the words they listed. If valuable vocabulary emerges, you may write new words on the board and students may make vocabulary cards (see page 61).

    > Online: Students return to the main room before sharing.

Variation: In another lesson, choose two pictures that are similar. For example, choose two pictures of chairs and ask, "How are these different?" This will generate words like "small" and "large," "old" and "new."

6.13 THE HOKEY POKEY

This playful song pumps up energy as everyone moves their body. Both children and adults enjoy it. Here are the words for the first verse of the song, "The Hokey Pokey." You can find the simple melody and a short video demonstration on the internet.

You put your right foot in,

You take your right foot out,

You put your right foot in,

And you shake it all about.

You do "The Hokey Pokey"

And you turn yourself around.

That's what it's all about!

 AIMS: Reviewing parts of the body, right and left, and the two-word verbs put in, take out, and turn around

Procedure:

1. Stand in a circle with your students.

   Online: Ask the students to stand up.

2. Demonstrate the song while students observe. While singing the song, do all the actions. As you sing, "You do the Hokey Pokey and you turn yourself around," wave your hands above your head and turn around. As you sing, "That's what it's all about!", clap your hands with the rhythm.

   You might want to show your students a video of this. It's easy to find online.

3. Students join you in the actions, singing along with as many words as they can. Repeat each line together until students are moving and singing with confidence.

   Online: Students put their body parts toward the camera rather than into the class circle.

4. Use other parts of the body (your hand, your elbow, etc.). This is a time to have fun and be silly. After reviewing the main parts of the body, try things like:

   "Put an eye in…"

   "Put your stomach in…"

   "Put your bottom in…"

5. Invite a volunteer to lead the singing and action, deciding what parts of the body to do.

6. Continue with other volunteers until parts of the body have been used many times.

7. To conclude the game, use this line: "Put your whole self in, take your whole self out." The motion here is a jump into and out of the circle.

Note: If you don't want to sing this, just do it as a chant or play the song from the web instead of singing it.

6.14 PLAYING WITH NUMBERS: WHAT ADDS UP TO 14?

Language learners often revert to saying numbers in their native language because those words are so deeply embedded in memory. This activity gives students plenty of practice saying numbers in their new language.

 AIM: Practicing numbers and math vocabulary such as "plus" and "equals"

Procedure:

1. Choose any two-digit number. If you choose 14, write this equation on the board:
   _____ + _____ = 14

2. Elicit from the class two numbers and write them in the blanks to finish the equation. Students repeat this chorally.

3. Ask for two different numbers that add up to 14 and write this new equation on the board.

4. In small groups, students write down more combinations they can think of whose total is 14. Examples: $10 + 4$, $7 + 7$, $13 + 1$, $14 + 0$.

> Online: Put a small group in each breakout room.

5. Call on any student to read out their number combinations while the class repeats each one chorally.

> Online: Students return to the main room before sharing.

6. Invite volunteers to share any combinations the first student missed. Again, the whole class repeats these chorally.

7. Continue the activity by choosing a different two-digit number.

Note: Play with subtraction, multiplication, and division as soon as your students are ready for more of a challenge. The point is to give students plenty of practice thinking about and saying numbers in English.

6.15 PLAYING WITH NUMBERS: STUDENTS MAKE THEIR OWN EQUATIONS

Students need plenty of practice using numbers in their new language. In this activity, they make their own equations to practice with numbers and the vocabulary of math.

 AIM: Practicing numbers and the words *plus*, *minus*, and *equals*

Procedure:

Demonstration:

1. Choose seven students to demonstrate what small groups will do. Each student gets ready to write on a paper large enough for the class to see.

2. Dictate three numbers to the first three students, e.g., 9, 7, and 3. Dictate three symbols to three other students: -, +, and =. Ask the seventh student to draw a blank line. Write on the board one possible equation with these elements, e.g., 9 + 7 - 3 = ____, to model what you are looking for.

3. Invite the students to decide together what equation they want to make. They may arrange their numbers and symbols in an equation different from the one you had in mind.

> Online: Put the seven students in a breakout room for a minute or two.

4. This demonstration group stands in order in front of the class. One by one, they read out their papers.

> Online: Students return to the main room. One student reads the whole equation to the class: for example, "seven minus three plus nine equals blank."

5. The class repeats the equation chorally and calls out the answer that should be in the blank.

6. To demonstrate how smaller groups can work, have some of the volunteer students give their paper to someone else in the group and sit down. Now there might be only four or five students standing in a row, some of them holding two papers with consecutive items from the equation.

> Online: Breakout groups with fewer than seven students complete the task just as before: by deciding collectively how to convert the seven "ingredients" into an equation that one group member will ultimately read to the class.

The Activity:

7. Time to play! Put students in groups of four to seven students, with seven in each group when possible.

Procedure (continued):

8. In each group, students create a new equation, choosing three random numbers and using the three symbols on the board. Students write these seven elements on their separate papers.

> Online: Put a small group in each breakout room to create an equation together. One member from each group shares their screen with their groupmates as they discuss how to make the equation.

9. Once every group has an equation, call on one group at a time to stand in a line in front of the class, showing their papers in order. As in the demonstration, students take turns reading the papers they are holding. The class repeats the equation chorally and calls out the solution at the end.

> Online: Students return to the main room. One member of each group shares their screen and reads out their equation for the class to repeat and solve.

Variation: For fun, invite groups to re-arrange themselves into new equations.

Extension: In a later class you might repeat this activity, including "times" and "divided by" to play with multiplication and division.

6.16 WHAT WE ALREADY KNOW ABOUT THIS

Why guess what students may or may not know before we start a lesson? They can tell us! In this activity, students offer ideas related to something you are about to teach.

 AIMS: Eliciting words and ideas students already know, activating students' background knowledge

Procedure:

1. Before a reading, listening passage, or discussion, ask "What do we already know about ___?"

2. As students call out ideas, list them on the board. Make sure everyone understands what you are writing.

3. Continue with your planned activity.

> This activity works equally well in an online class with no adaptations.

6.17 FOUR CORNERS VOCABULARY

In this activity, students create associations, including pictures, for their new words. This process connects new words and their meanings to several areas of the brain.

 AIM: Remembering new words in three different ways

Procedure:

1. Individually, students make a four-square table for each new word.

> Online: Students will create their tables in a document.

2. Ask students to write in the first quadrant a word they have learned recently. In the second quadrant, they draw a picture of something they associate with this word. In the third quadrant, they write a translation. In the fourth quadrant, they write a sentence using the word in context. They may glance at classmates' papers or ask for help if they need it.

Word	Picture
Translation	Context Sentence

3. One way to play with these is for a student to show the class their illustration in quadrant 2. Classmates guess the word

> Online: Students can share their screen and zoom in on quadrant 2.

Acknowledgement: We adapted this from trainers of the SIOP method. Thank you very much!

STAGE 3 - MAKE THE WORDS MY OWN

6.18 USE IT BEFORE I SLEEP

In this activity, students use new words in real contexts in their own lives. They get very creative in finding ways to use a new word! For instance, a student might talk about their family in their native language at suppertime and drop in the English word "brother" just for fun. The mental process of creating ways to use a new word is an excellent way to anchor the word in their memory. This may be the best strategy known to humankind for "deep learning" of vocabulary.

 AIM: Anchoring words in long-term memory

Procedure:

1. After learning a new word, students make a point of using it in conversation outside class.

2. They report back in the next class about how they used the word.

> This activity works equally well in an online class with no adaptations.

6.19 WHAT AM I DRAWING?

This fast-paced drawing activity is a real class pleaser! From a student's drawing, other students guess a word the class has been studying. As they play with each word, they are also bringing in the grammar they have learned. One final benefit: students create original sentences using the words.

You can play this with the whole class or as a team or pair game.

 AIMS: Recycling and expanding previously taught vocabulary, using multiple intelligences

MATERIALS: A vocabulary list based on a certain theme or aspect of language such as nouns, action verbs, irregular verbs, emotions, or any words your students have studied

Procedure:

1. Give the students a list of words. If your students are low beginners, use nouns because they're easier to draw and guess. Less concrete words, like adjectives or irregular past tense verbs, are more fun but also more challenging.

> Online: Make the list of words available on your course site.

Procedure (continued):

2. Choose a volunteer who likes to draw. This student joins you at the board to draw a word you point to from the list. Key point: They must not speak or gesture!

> Online: Send the volunteer a message in the chat telling them which word to draw. They will share their screen and draw the word using the "annotate"/"draw" feature.

3. The student continues drawing until a classmate guesses the word.

4. The person who guesses correctly gets one point. They get more points if they can expand on the word in some way. For example, if you are using a list of irregular past tense verbs like "went," a student will try to draw the idea of "going." A classmate who guesses by saying "go" gets one point. If they can say "went," they get two points. If they say an original sentence with "went," they get three points. Other classmates can earn points by helping if needed.

   If you are using a list of adjectives, students get one point for the word "old," two points for saying its opposite, "young," and three points for using it correctly in a sentence.

   Note: To increase speaking time, the class chorally repeats each correct sentence.

5. Choose a new volunteer and give them a new word to draw. Continue the game as long as students are having fun.

6.20 STUDENT-RUN VOCABULARY REVIEW

We always have a few students who have learned certain words quickly and well. This activity gives them a chance to shine as they help their classmates review words they're learning.

 AIM: Reviewing vocabulary, students helping students

Procedure:

1. As a vocabulary review, write on the board some words you taught recently that some students may need help with.

2. Read them aloud. Students repeat each word chorally.

3. Invite a few volunteers to come up and write their name by a word they know well enough to use easily in conversation.

> Online: Students can write the word in the chat.

4. One at a time, students re-teach their word to the rest of the class using at least one example sentence with the word. If there are multiple student volunteers for a given word, you may elicit an example sentence from each of those students.

Procedure (continued):

5. In small groups, students create a new original sentence for each of the words their classmates just taught.

> Online: Put a small group in each breakout room.

6. As a class, volunteers offer some of the sentences their group created.

> Online: Students return to the main room before sharing.

6.21 CREATING NEW STORIES WITH OUR WORDS

As your students master more and more words, you can offer the challenge of creating stories that use them. These stories can be fiction or non-fiction, personal or not. This activity works well in multi-level classes. Many students may work on their own, using words they feel confident with. Students who want some support may work in pairs or small groups.

 AIM: Reviewing words by creating original stories that use them

Procedure:

1. Students work individually, in pairs, or in small groups to create a story using as many of their new words as they can.

> Online: If students are not working individually, put a pair or small group in each breakout room.

2. Volunteers read their stories out loud to the class. If they want to, they can announce how many new words they used. You might lead the class in applauding each story.

> Online: If students were working in pairs or groups, they return to the main room before sharing.

3. (Optional) Students may post their stories in or outside the classroom for others to enjoy reading.

> Online: Students can post their stories on the discussion board.

Chapter Seven

Grammar

When we approach a new language, the new words and sounds seem complex and tangled. Grammar helps to make sense of it all. Students see how their own languages are similar to the target language and how they are different. They learn how to ask a question, form a negative sentence, and put words in an order that their listeners can understand. In short, lots of practice with putting words together into a meaningful structure helps students to learn, to remember, and to communicate.

The activities in this chapter offer options for low and more advanced beginners. These strategies will help all of your students feel at home in the structures of their new language.

7.1 TELL IT LIKE IT ISN'T

Students can laugh at the teacher's mistakes in this lively activity. It also generates a nice list of action verbs to add to students' vocabulary collection.

 AIM: Practicing the present continuous tense, action verbs, and negation

Procedure:

1. Take a student where the class can't see or hear you. Whisper to them to act out an action such as "Eat a sandwich."

    > Online: Put one student in a breakout room and join them to show what they will do. (You may also be able to give the students instructions by simply using the chat.)

2. As the student mimes for the class, say, "Evandro is driving a car. Right?" Write "drive" on the board as you say this.

    > Online: Both of you return to the main room before the student acts out the action.

3. Elicit from students, "No, he is not driving a car. He is eating a sandwich." Write "eat" on the board.

4. Take a different student aside and coach them to do a new action. (Possibilities include eating, drinking, cooking, brushing teeth, sleeping, driving, reading, writing, taking a shower, walking, etc.)

    > Online: As in Step 1, put one student in a breakout room and join them to show what they will do.

5. Repeat with more students. Each time, suggest the wrong verb and have the class correct you with the verb that's being mimed. Write both verbs on the board as you go along. Note: Encourage students to collect useful new words throughout your course. See Vocabulary Cards (page 61) for one effective way to do this.

7.2 MAKE QUESTIONS FOR THE ANSWERS

After students know some wh-question words, students see answers and create original wh-questions to match. It's a fun way to review and practice wh-question formation while learning more about their classmates.

 AIMS: Reviewing wh-question formation, building class cohesion

Procedure:

Demonstration:

1. Write your name on the board along with some possible answers to questions about yourself. For example, "Michal, two, Maryland, in the morning." These answers could include your age, the place you were born, the number of years you have been a teacher, and the names of your children. Use your imagination.

2. Point to one fact on the board and say, "Here is an answer to a question about me. What is a good question for this answer?"

3. Volunteers suggest possible questions. For example, if you pointed to "two," a question might be "How many children do you have?" Write this on the board, circling the question words "How many." The class repeats the question.

4. Repeat the procedure, circling each question word until you have several answers and their questions on the board. Help with corrections as needed and do plenty of choral repetition.

Students Get to Work:

5. Point to each question word you circled in Step 3 as students say them chorally. Your question words might include *who*, *what*, *where*, *when*, and *how many*.

6. Students take a few minutes to write their name and some answers about themselves on a piece of paper. They give this to the teacher.

> Online: Students write this in the chat.

7. Choose one answer that will elicit a question with *when*, such as "yesterday" or "everyday. Show Haiyan's answer to the class.

8. In small groups, students write a few questions beginning with *when* about Haiyan's answer.

> Online: Put a pair in each breakout room.

9. A volunteer offers a question. If it is grammatically correct, praise this student. Then let Haiyan tell whether this question is the one she was thinking of. If it is not, more classmates can offer different questions for her answer. It's fun, and they are getting plenty of practice with *when*.

> Online: Students return to the main room before sharing.

10. Choose a different answer from a different student, perhaps one that will elicit questions with *what*. Continue the activity with other question words.

7.3 SENTENCE EXPANSION

This playful activity helps students write more interesting, detailed sentences. It's also a holistic way to practice many grammatical structures; they learn without needing grammatical labels.

It's fun because many of our students have excellent memorization skills. They love the challenge of remembering the long sentence they're creating together.

 AIMS: Practicing structures, forming correct sentences, adding details to writing

Procedure:

1. Put a simple sentence on the board – for example, "Fatima buys vegetables." Spread the words out on the board so there is a lot of empty space to fill in.

2. Every student thinks of a word or phrase that can be added and raises their hand. Note: When we ask for volunteers, some students never get the chance to do the important mental processing that makes this activity valuable.

3. Call on a student for their suggestion. Make sure they say the whole sentence, including their addition, e.g., "Fatima buys vegetables and chicken."

4. Ask the class whether this addition is grammatically possible and makes sense. If so, write it in or invite a student to do this. Then have the whole class repeat the ever-growing sentence chorally. Note: Step 4 is the heart of the activity. Students are exploring what can and cannot be done with a sentence.

5. Continue the activity, accepting contributions until you decide the sentence is as long as it can get. If students run out of ideas too soon, prompt them with questions such as "Where?", "When?", "Why?", "How?", "How many?", "How much?", "What kind of?", "How often?", "Who else?", and "What else?"

6. By the end, the whole class may be repeating something like "Every week, Fatima and her husband take a bus to the grocery store on Hill Street and buy vegetables, chicken, apples, and laundry detergent, but last week they forgot to buy milk."

This activity works equally well in an online class with no adaptations.

7.4 SENTENCE CONTRACTION

This simple activity helps students understand sentence structure by finding the "skeleton" of a sentence. There is usually more than one correct way to trim a sentence down to its basic elements. In the process, students learn a lot about grammar and punctuation.

 AIMS: Identifying the main clause in a sentence, analyzing and manipulating grammatical structures

Procedure:

1. Write on the board a long sentence with vocabulary your students are already familiar with. For example, you might write, "My grandmother, who lived in New York, smoked cigarettes every morning and every afternoon of her life, but to my surprise she lived to be ninety years old."

2. Ask students, "What can we take away and still have a correct sentence?"

3. Every student chooses a word or phrase that can be removed and raises their hand. Note: When we ask for volunteers, some students never get the chance to do the important mental processing that makes this activity valuable.

4. Call on a student for their suggestion, putting parentheses around that word or phrase on the board. Ask the class whether this deletion leaves a sentence that is grammatically correct and makes sense. If that deletion works, erase what is in parentheses.

5. The whole class repeats this shorter sentence chorally.

6. Continue calling on students until the sentence is as simple as it can be. Feel free to change words a bit to get down to the absolute "skeleton" of the sentence. For example, your class might end with, "My grandmother smoked cigarettes but lived to be old."

This activity works equally well in an online class with no adaptations.

7.5 SUBSTITUTION DRILLS

With Substitution Drills, students think fast to change elements of a sentence based on cues you give them. They are a great way to play with any grammar or vocabulary you've been working on. See the example list in the "Teacher" column below.

Substitution Drills take a bit of practice at first, but they are worth it. Once you and your students find your rhythm, you will want to use them again and again!

AIM: Reviewing grammatical structures

SETUP: Write a list of the cues you will use to give your class practice with structures they've been learning.

Procedure:

1.   Dictate your first sentence. The class repeats it chorally.

2.   Dictate one change at time. As a class, students say the revised sentence. Note: If some students are getting it wrong, just gesture for the whole class to say it again. As they listen to one another, more and more students will be saying the correctly revised sentence.

It's easy to adapt substitution drills for different levels in your classes. For a group of low beginners, you might change just one element at a time.

Teacher	Class
Yoshiko got up at 7:00.	Yoshiko got up at 7:00.
8:00	Yoshiko got up at **8:00.**
Marco	**Marco** got up at 8:00.
(Continue with more changes.)	(The class says the revised sentences.)

If your students are a little more advanced, you might change an element that requires the students to make more than one change in the sentence.

Teacher	Class
Maria drives her car to school.	Maria drives her car to school.
Ali	**Ali** drives **his** car to school.
Abdu and Abeke	**Abdu and Abeke drive their** car to school.
grocery store	Abdu and Abeke drive their car to **the grocery store.**
truck	Abdu and Abeke drive their **truck** to the grocery store.
yesterday	Abdu and Abeke **drove** their truck to the grocery store **yesterday.**
(Continue with more changes.)	(The class says the revised sentences.)

This activity works equally well in an online class with no adaptations.

7.6 TRUTH OR CHAIR?

Students laugh a lot as they walk around giving accurate and inaccurate names to objects and correcting each other.

AIMS: Practicing affirmative and negative sentences with the verb "to be," practicing *this* vs. *that* (see extension), reviewing names of objects

SETUP: If you are teaching online, post on your course site a picture with many classroom objects.

Procedure:

Demonstration:

1. Walk around pointing to objects in the room and saying, for example, "This is a window/a chair/a shoe/etc." Students repeat your statements chorally. Pre-teach vocabulary if necessary.

> Online: Share your screen to show the picture you posted. Circle each object as you say it. Then erase the circles.

2. Write on the board:

   • This is a _____.

   • Yes, this is a _____.

   Every student copies these two sentence frames on a piece of paper. The class practices saying them chorally.

3. Stand with a volunteer student near a window (for example). Point to the window and say, "This is a window." Prompt the student to respond, "Yes, this is a window." Visit a few more objects and take turns saying the two sentences.

> Online: Share your screen to show the picture you posted. Circle one object at a time for them to practice with.

To Practice Affirmative Statements:

4. Erase the two sentence frames from the board. Students pair up and walk around, holding their papers behind their backs. They take turns pointing out objects and saying the two sentences. They may bring their papers out for a quick glance if needed, but make sure they don't speak while looking at their papers.

> Online: Put a pair in each breakout room. One student shares their screen to show a picture (from what you posted or another image). They use the draw tool to identify one object at a time.

5. Instruct students to alternate so they each practice both sentences. When you feel they've practiced enough, invite them to return to their seats.

> Online: Students return to the main room.

Procedure (continued):

To Practice Negative Statements:

6. Demonstrate the activity again, this time with negatives. This is where it really becomes fun! Write on the board:

    • "This is a _____."

    • "No, this isn't a _____! It's a _____."

    Every student copies these two new sentence frames on a piece of paper. The class practices saying them chorally.

    To demonstrate, stand near the window again with a different student. Point to it and say, "This is a door." Prompt the student to respond, "No, this isn't a door! It's a window!" Demonstrate with a few more examples, taking turns so you each use both sentences. Each time, be sure to stand near the object because you are using *this*.

    > Online: Share your screen again to show the picture you posted. Circle one object at a time for this demonstration.

7. Erase the two sentence frames from the board. Again, students pair up and walk around, holding their papers behind their backs. This time they take turns pointing to something and saying it is something that it is NOT. At this point, they may not need to refer to their papers.

    > Online: Put a pair in each breakout room.

8. Continue as long as students are having fun.

Extension using *this* and *that*: With more advanced beginners, they may touch a door and say, for example, "This is a window." Their partner points to a window and replies, "No, this isn't a window. THIS is a door. THAT is a window."

Acknowledgment: We learned this from Tessa Woodward, at the Pilgrims' Language School in Canterbury, England.

Supercharge Your Teaching!

"Truth or Chair?" features students' keeping a sheet with the needed phrases close by if they need a reminder. You'll find more information about this strategy ("Papers Behind Our Backs") and other tips, in our free guide *Supercharge Your Teaching*, downloadable from ProLinguaLearning.com/resources.

7.7 BUILDING DIALOGUES ABOUT FOOD

We all enjoy good food. This activity helps students bring some of that enjoyment into their new language while practicing basic grammar and learning about one another's likes and dislikes.

 AIMS: Practicing yes/no questions and negatives using *like* and *don't like*, practicing the pronouns *he*, *she*, and *they*, using the third person singular "s"

Procedure:

1. Write on the board the names of several foods students are familiar with. Include some that students probably don't like. You might choose foods such as apples, garlic, carrots, raw onions, bread, old cheese, pizza, cold soup, hamburger, hot spices, chocolate, or nuts.

2. Put these three sentence frames on the board:

   • Do you like _____?

   • Yes, I like _____.

   • No, I don't like ____.

   Every student copies the sentence frames on a piece of paper. The class practices by saying them chorally.

3. Ask, for example, "Lucia, do you like bread?" The class repeats her answer chorally, "Lucia likes bread," or "Lucia doesn't like bread."

4. Do this with a few students. The first time you get a negative answer with a third-person singular or plural subject, write it on the board as an additional example sentence. For example, write, "She doesn't like bread.", "He doesn't like bread.", and "They don't like bread." Students copy these onto their paper and practice them chorally a few times.

5. Erase the four sentences from the board. Students stand and mingle, asking one classmate at a time questions about foods and answering the questions. They hide their sentence-prompt papers, bringing them out for a quick glance if needed. Make sure they don't speak while looking at their papers.

   > Online: Put a pair in each breakout room.

6. You might circulate among students, listening for correct questions and answers. Continue as long as there is interest.

7. After the mingle, ask everyone, "Who remembers what Francisco likes?" A volunteer answers, "He likes_____." The class repeats this chorally. This lets everyone practice pronouns and the third-person singular "s."

   > Online: Students return to the main room before sharing.

7.8 WHAT DO WE DO? PRACTICING SHORT ANSWERS WITH *DO* AND *DOES*

Students need a great deal of practice with short yes/no answers and negatives. This activity is a fun way to play with these. As a bonus, students learn more about their classmates. This activity uses the same grammar as "Building Dialogues About Food" (page 83) and adds more verbs to the mix.

 AIMS: Using yes/no questions with *do* and *does*, practicing short answers and negatives

Procedure:

1. Write on the board these sentence frames:
   - Questions: Do you ___? Does he/she _____?
   - Answers: Yes, he/she does.   No, he/she doesn't.

   Note: If some students are using gender-neutral pronouns, include "Yes, they do." "No, they don't."

2. Describe yourself by saying, for example, "I am a teacher. I do many things. I teach English. I cook food. I ride a bicycle," As you talk, mime each action and write the verbs on the board under your name.

3. Ask one student, for example, "Mohammed, do you speak Arabic?" Elicit his answer and repeat it, "Mohammed speaks Arabic."

4. Ask the class, "Does Mohammed speak Arabic?" Teach the phrase, "Yes, he does" and write it on the board.

5. Elicit a few more answers from Mohammed about what he does. As you go along, write the simple form of each verb under Mohammed's name on the board. Ask the class, for example, "Does Mohammed study?" Students chorally repeat, "Yes, he does." Do this with a few more verbs about what Mohammed does.

6. Call on a student of a different gender and ask what they do, writing a few verbs under their name. You might ask, "Does Natalia walk to school?" The class continues choral repetition, this time with "Yes, she does." Continue with two or three more students, adding their names and verbs to the board. Be sure to choose a few verbs that may not be true for everybody. You'll need these in the next step.

7. Now you can practice with negative answers! For example, you might ask, "Mohammed speaks Arabic. Does Natalia speak Arabic?" As you ask question after question, the class repeats, "No, he/she doesn't." or "No, they don't."

8. For independent practice, students look at the names and verbs on the board and quiz each other about classmates.

> Online: Put a pair in each breakout room. Post the document with the names and verbs on your course site (or share it in some other way) so the students can access it in the breakout room.

Extension: In a later class, you might repeat this activity with different students' names and verbs on the board.

7.9 CLEANING UP THE MESS

Students need a great deal of practice with short yes/no answers and negatives. Everyone knows what a joy it is to get one's messy room cleaned up. In this activity, students practice the simple past tense while describing the clean-up.

AIMS: Practicing simple past tense verbs, generating vocabulary

SETUP: For online classes, post a copy of the two pictures on your course site (or share them in some other way).

Procedure:

1. Show the class the picture of the messy room. Write on the board several nouns about what you and your students see there.

   > Online: Share your screen to show the picture.

2. Next, show the picture of the clean room and ask the class, "What did someone do?" Write some past tense verbs and nouns on the board in sentences such as "They picked up the book." "They put away the shoes." "They watered the flower." "They made the bed." and "They fixed the picture." Students repeat each sentence chorally.

3. Have students copy the sentences to practice writing. Then erase the board.

4. In pairs, students take turns saying the sentences to each other. Make sure students keep their papers behind their backs. They can see the pictures but should glance briefly at their papers only if they need to.

   > Online: Put a pair in each breakout room.

5. Volunteers may share sentences that were not on the board about the pictures.

   > Online: Students return to the main room before sharing.

Extension: Students may offer sentences about something they cleaned up or organized in the recent past.

7.10 WHAT KIND OF NOUN IS THIS?

In this activity, students discover the four common categories of nouns and play with using them where nouns typically occur in sentences.

AIMS: Learning what a noun is, using nouns correctly in sentences

Procedure:

1. Ask the class, "What are some examples of nouns?" Prompt contributions by saying, "What are more words like cat, girl, student, or book?"

2. Write on the board a table like the one below, but with words contributed by you and your students.

PERSON	PLACE	THING	IDEA
teacher	city	bus	love
student	school	house	fear
doctor	hospital	cup	freedom
Maria	supermarket	arm	truth
man	New York	sandwich	life

3. Continue encouraging responses or supplying nouns until you have words in all four columns: person, place, thing, and idea.

4. To practice where nouns typically occur in sentences, write on the board sentence frames such as

   - "___ is good."
   - "I gave the ___ to _____."
   - "I gave ____ the ____."
   - "I don't like ____."

5. Elicit nouns to complete one sentence at a time and write them on the board. The class chorally repeats good sentences.

6. Individually, students write several sentences of their own.

7. In small groups, students tell their partners what they wrote.

   > Online: Put a pair in each breakout room.

8. A few volunteers tell the class one sentence they heard from a partner.

   > Online: Students return to the main room before sharing.

See 2.1 "Popcorn Listening" (Chapter 2, page 10) for a holistic way to learn all the parts of speech.

7.11 PLAYING WITH WH-QUESTIONS

Students think fast as they practice the meanings of question words by matching them with appropriate answers. This activity works well after students have a basic understanding of the individual question words. It will help you and your students discover which question words they know well and which ones they need to practice more.

 AIMS: Understanding and reviewing wh-question words and appropriate responses, creating original wh-questions

Procedure:

1. Write on the board these four information question words: *who, what, where,* and *when.* Teach the meanings if necessary.

2. Write on the board in random order several answers that will match *who, what, where,* and *when.* For example, you might write, "at 3:00," "at home," "apples," "my teacher," "at the store," "my friend," "in the morning," and "book."

3. Point to one of the answers. In pairs, students choose one of the four question words and create an original question for this answer.

   > Online: Put a pair in each breakout room.

4. Both partners practice saying their sentence out loud to each other. Then they raise their hands together.

   > Online: Students return to the main room.

5. Call on a partner from one of the early pairs. If their sentence is incorrect, classmates offer help. If their sentence is correct, the class repeats it chorally.

6. That pair chooses a different answer from the board, and every pair gets back to work making a new question.

   > Online: Put a pair in the breakout room. You can shuffle the breakout rooms if you want to.

7. Continue the activity, adding new answer words if you need more, until students are using these question words with confidence.

Extension: Once students have demonstrated that they have mastered these four question words, teach *why* and *how* or *how many* and *how much.*

7.12 THINK FAST! PRACTICING VERB TENSES

Being able to say new sentences on the spur of the moment gives students a real sense of accomplishment.

 AIM: Reviewing verb tenses, creating original sentences

Procedure:

1. Write on the board a few verb tenses you want to review, for example, simple present, simple past, present continuous.

2. Choose a verb that students know well such as *eat*. To demonstrate what students will do in pairs, call out the verb and point to one of the tenses named on the board. Invite two volunteers to talk to each other and create a sentence using *eat* in that verb tense. When each of them has helped their partner practice the sentence, they are both ready to speak: they raise their hands together at the same time and look at you. Call on one of them. When you get a correct sentence, the class repeats it chorally.

> Online: The two volunteers quickly share ideas and create a sentence together in a private chat. When they have both practiced saying that sentence, they both use the raised-hand icon.

3. Now the fun begins! Tell students they will be working in pairs to create sentence after sentence on command as you name a verb and point to a tense.

4. Call out a verb and point to a tense. When both students have practiced a sentence, pairs raise their hands together. Call on a member of an early-finishing pair. If they immediately say a correct sentence, the class repeats this chorally. Then name another verb and tense for pairs to work with. If a student doesn't have an answer ready, say to that pair, "Oh, you're not quite ready to speak." Ask all of the pairs to take a few moments and practice again so everyone is ready to speak. The next time, everyone will make sure they have practiced sufficiently with their partner the first time.

> Online: Put a pair in each breakout room. Send them a message in the chat with the verb and the tense you want them to use. When both partners have practiced saying a sentence, they return to the main room. After a few pairs arrive, bring everyone back and call on a member of an early pair. If that student has a good sentence ready, the class repeats it. If they have trouble, call on another pair. (It may not be worth the time in an online setting to put the students back in their breakout room, as we suggest in an in-person setting.)

5. Repeat this, keeping the pace quick. Beginners need a lot of repetition for deep learning, and the pace will pick up as everyone gets used to this activity.

Variation: You can use this routine – giving a prompt and expecting a series of quick responses – to practice many different grammar points. Have fun with it!

7.13 THIS IS MY ELEPHANT

We can make repetition fun by changing a sentence frame in a chain, one student at a time. In addition, using real objects makes learning memorable! In this activity, students practice how to talk about ownership.

AIMS: Practicing the possessive pronouns *this* and *that* and the possessive adjectives *my, your, his, her,* and *their*

SETUP: Ask students to bring an object big enough for everyone to see. It should be one they know the name of. Bring one for yourself. Stuffed animals are fun because they are playful!

Procedure:

1. Everyone, including you, names their object, holding it up for all to see. If the name of an object is new to some students, teach it.

2. Say to the class, for example, "This is my elephant." Point to the object that a student is holding and say, "That is your monkey." You may need to teach *my* and *your* to get them started.

3. Repeat, "This is my elephant. That is your monkey."

4. Ask the student, "What is that?" The student answers, "This is my monkey." If the student doesn't know the word *this*, invite classmates to help them.

5. Holding up your elephant, ask the same student, "What is this?" The student answers, "That is your elephant."

6. Coach this the same student to start a chain by saying say, "This is my monkey." Gesturing to a classmate, they ask, "What is that?"

7. Their classmate answers, "This is my _____. That is your _____." They immediately turn to a third classmate and ask, "What is that?".

8. Continue the chain with each successive student using the three sentences in Step 7 until students are speaking fluently.

Extension: To add *his, her,* and *their* to the chain, point to one student's object and ask the class, "What is that?" Students answer chorally, "That is her / his / their _____." You may need to teach these words. Point to other students' objects and let the class tell you what they are, using *his, her, their, my,* and *your* until all students are succeeding.

This activity works equally well in an online class with no adaptations.

7.14 WEEKLY ROUTINES

In this activity, students interview one another about what they do regularly. After they've spoken to a few partners, they report to the class what they've learned. Unlike the simpler activity "What I Eat, What You Eat" in Chapter 3 (page 28), this activity lets students use a lot of different verbs and gives them practice with questions.

 AIMS: Practicing information questions with *what*, using the simple present tense, learning about classmates

Procedure:

1. Write on the board, "What do you do every week?" Write a true answer, for example, "I clean my house."

2. Ask, "What do you do every week?" Elicit a few answers. Volunteers call out two or three things they do every week.

3. Erase your personal answer. What remains on the board is the interview students will use.

   • Student 1: "What do you do every week?"

   • Student 2: "I _____."

4. Call on two students to demonstrate the interview. As you coach each student to speak, the class chorally repeats the question and the answer.

5. Students copy the model interview from the board. On the same paper, they write two or three things they do.

6. Erase the model interview. Practice the model a few more times, chorally and individually, until students are speaking confidently.

7. Students mingle, interviewing each other in pairs to find out what their classmates typically do. Make sure they have put away their interview paper. They may glance at it if they need to, but they must hide it again before speaking to each partner.

   > Online: Put a small group in each breakout room. After a short time, shuffle the breakout rooms.

8. Ask the class, "Who remembers something about somebody?" Students call out what they remember. For fun, you might write on the board, "Me, too!" and "So do I!" and encourage the class to use these two phrases.

   > Online: Students return to the main room before sharing.

Extension: Do this activity with other tenses, asking "What did you do last week?" or "What will you do next week?"

7.15 PREPOSITION PICTURES

This activity enlists peer support in using prepositions of place correctly. Drawing pictures reinforces learning. Don't worry if some students say they can't draw; just put some very basic stick figures on the board and tell them, "If you can do this, it's fine!"

 AIM: Practicing prepositions of place

Procedure:

1. Dictate one sentence at a time using a preposition of place. For example: "The monkey is on the box."

2. Each student draws what they hear.

3. Students look at a few classmates' pictures. If they want to, they may change their drawing.

> Online: Students hold their picture up to the camera.

4. Each student individually writes under their picture the sentence as they remember it. Then they may help each other revise what they wrote.

> Online: Students can write their sentence in the chat or share their screen to show the sentence.

5. A volunteer shares their picture and sentence. The class offers help if needed.

Extension: In another lesson, do this activity using other prepositions.

7.16 SCRAMBLING WORDS IN A SENTENCE

Some languages, including English, depend heavily on word order. In this fun activity, students put words in the right order to make correct sentences. It's self-corrected, giving each student individualized feedback about grammar.

AIMS: Practicing word order in sentences

MATERIALS: Sentences your students are familiar with

SETUP: For online classes, post on your course site two separate documents, each with a few sentences. Label one Document A and the other Document B.

Procedure:

1. Choose two sentences your students are familiar with. Half of your students will write down one of the sentences, and the other half will write the other sentence. Choose two volunteers and give one sentence to each volunteer to dictate to half of the class. One group can step outside the classroom or go to a corner to keep what they are dictating a secret from the other half of the class.

> Online: Put a pair in each breakout room. They decide who is A and who is B. Instruct the A students to look at Document A, and the B students to look at Document B. They will use the sentences in these documents to create their sentence scrambles.

2. Each student cuts or tears their words apart and scrambles them.

> Online: Students rearrange the words of their sentence in random order.

3. Students trade their sets of words and re-assemble their partner's sentence. Encourage them to do this on their own without asking their partner for help.

> Online: Students share their screen to show their partners the words each of them scrambled (or they can share their lists of scrambled words in the chat). They each make a new document to turn their partner's scrambled words into a sentence.

4. When both partners have reassembled their scrambled words, they check each other's work and offer suggestions if needed.

5. Show everyone the two original sentences for a final confirmation.

> Online: Students look at both sets of sentences you posted.

6. Repeat with two new sentences and continue as long as students are engaged.

7.17 VOCABULARY CHAIN

Challenge can be fun! In this activity, students need to concentrate because they have to remember what classmates have said. In the example below, students are practicing the simple past tense. You can use this routine with any content.

 AIMS: Reinforcing grammar by adapting a sentence frame many times, listening closely to remember what classmates have said, using classmates' names

Procedure:

1. Students sit in a circle of no more than fifteen. In large classes, make more than one circle.

> Online: Students don't sit in a circle.

2. Choose a sentence to start the chain. For example, say, "Last Saturday, I saw a movie."

3. Say, "Yuji, what did I do?" He answers, "You saw a movie." Ask him what he did and help him form a complete sentence. Yuji repeats both sentences: "You saw a movie. I went shopping." The class repeats this chorally.

4. Call on the student next to Yuji. Prompt them to repeat what you did and what Yuji did and add their own answer. They might say, for example, "Michal saw a movie. Yuji went shopping. I worked." Each time a student adds their sentence, the class repeats this growing chain chorally.

5. Continue calling on students. If someone doesn't remember a classmate's answer, they may call for help from the class.

6. Everyone applauds the last student, who has the hardest job!

7. As a class, students say the entire chain one last time. Congratulate them!

Variations: This activity is very flexible. You can build up a chain using other verb tenses or you can practice colors and clothing words by starting with a sentence like, "Today, I am wearing black pants."

Acknowledgment: We learned this activity from Ellen Abrams, a teacher of art and Spanish.

7.18 WHEN SUDDENLY...

The past continuous and simple past tenses are natural partners! Using them together makes it clear what each tense is for. In this playful activity, students finish sentences started by the teacher and then use both tenses to create their own original sentences.

 AIM: Practicing the past continuous and simple past tenses

Procedure:

1. Tell the class, "I'm going to tell you about something I did last weekend." Begin a sentence using the past continuous tense by saying, for example, "I was walking in the mountains, when suddenly. . ." Pause for drama. Provide an interesting conclusion using the simple past tense, perhaps "...a bear ran in front of me."

2. The class repeats the whole sentence.

3. Start a new sentence using a different verb in the past continuous tense. This time, a volunteer student offers a conclusion, again using the simple past tense. If this is correct, the class repeats the whole sentence. If it's not, classmates can offer help.

4. Continue starting new sentences. Invite volunteers to offer several ways to finish each sentence. The class repeats these.

5. With the class, you may discuss these two tenses and when to use them, e.g., "We use the past continuous tense when a longer-lasting action in the past is interrupted by a short action." Drawing a timeline can help students visualize this.

6. When students are ready, put them in small groups to make three sentences like the ones they've been practicing. Show them a model sentence and invite them to use different verbs to write original sentences.

Online: Put a small group in each breakout room.

7. Call on someone from each group to share one or more of their sentences.

Online: Students return to the main room before sharing.

INDEX OF ACTIVITY FUNCTIONS/TOPICS

These headings will help you find just the activity you need today.

1. ASSESSMENT: ERROR CORRECTION

We can always collect students' work when we need to give them grades. However, we know that when students correct their own work immediately, they learn more. Here are a few of the many activities throughout this book that lend themselves to one or both of these ways of correcting errors.

2.5 Active True/False 14

3.8 Homework or Quiz Review: Seek and Find 27

5.8 Editing and Revision: I Can Do It Myself 49

2. COMMUNITY-BUILDING ACTIVITIES

When students know each other well, they are less nervous about making mistakes and more ready to communicate in their new language. These activities help!

1.5 What's in My Wallet? 4

1.7 Taking Surveys 5

1.8 Offering Tea 6

3.2 What I Need 21

3.4 What's Your Name? Nice to Meet You 23

3.9 What I Eat, What You Eat 28

6.6 Getting to Know You: A Birthday Game 60

7.2 Make Questions for the Answers 77

7.7 Building Dialogues About Food 83

7.14 Weekly Routines 90

3. DIALOGUES

These activities give students a head start on their conversation skills.

2.3 Using the Telephone 12

7.6 Truth or Chair? 81

7.7 Building Dialogues About Food 83

7.8 What Do We Do? Practicing Short Answers with Do and Does..... 84

7.14 Weekly Routines 90

4. DRAWING

Drawing allows students to demonstrate comprehension when they aren't yet ready to speak much.

2.8 Picture Dictation 17

4.6 Add a Picture 36

6.19 What Am I Drawing? 72

7.15 Preposition Pictures 91

5. ENERGIZERS

When students are tired, try these activities to add some energy to your lessons!

1.3 Dance Party 3

1.7 Taking Surveys 5

2.1 Popcorn Listening 10

2.5 Active True/False 14

3.7 Let's Put on a Play! 26

4.2 On the Wall Outside 31

4.4 Students Choose Who's Next 34

6.13 The Hokey Pokey 67

6.15 Playing with Numbers: Students Make Their Own Equations 69

7.1 Tell It Like It Isn't 76

7.6 Truth or Chair? 81

6. FEEDBACK BUILT INTO THE LESSON

Students want to "get it right." Many Zero Prep activities are carefully crafted so that ongoing feedback is built right into the activity. Here are a few of those activities.

2.2 Singing Dictation: Building Up a Song 11

2.7 Catch the Teacher's Mistakes 16

2.8 Picture Dictation 17

2.9 Gossip 18

5.3 Let's Find Some Useful Mistakes 44

5.9 Spelling Improvement 51

7.11 Playing with Wh-Questions 87

7.12 Think Fast! Practicing Verb Tenses 88

7. FIRST FEW DAYS

People new to a language may have some anxieties about it. These activities are low-stress and build students' confidence in their ability to learn this new language.

1.9 What Day Is It Today? 6

3.1 Classroom Language 20

3.4 What's Your Name? Nice To Meet You! 23

3.5 Please and Thank You 23

5.3 Let's Find Some Useful Mistakes 44

6.7 Vocabulary Cards 61

6.9 All the Words We Know 63

8. GRAMMAR

Throughout the book, students are using grammar holistically. These headings will direct you to some discrete grammar points.

Affirmative and Negative Statements

7.1 Tell It Like It Isn't 76

7.6 Truth or Chair? 81

7.7 Building Dialogues About Food 83

7.8 What Do We Do? Practicing Short Answers with Do and Does..... 84

Nouns

7.10 What Kind of Noun is This? 86

Possessive Pronouns and Possessive Adjectives

7.13 This is My Elephant 89

Prepositions

2.8 Picture Dictation 17

7.15 Preposition Pictures 91

Question Formation

7.2 Make Questions for the Answers 77

7.7 Building Dialogues About Food 83

7.8 What Do We Do? Practicing Short Answers with Do and Does..... 84

7.11 Playing with Wh-Questions 87

7.14 Weekly Routines 90

Verb Tenses

7.1 Tell It Like It Isn't (Present Continuous) 76

7.12 Think Fast! Practicing Verb Tenses (all tenses) 88

7.17 Vocabulary Chain (all tenses) 93

7.18 When Suddenly... (past continuous and simple past)............. 94

Word Order

7.16 Scrambling Words in a Sentence 92

9. HIGH BEGINNERS

Many activities can be done with each student working at their own level in a multi-level class. If you have high beginners, check these out!

6.12 Two Unrelated Pictures: How Are They the Same? 66

7.2 Make Questions for the Answers 77

7.5 Substitution Drills (Option 2) 80

7.11 Playing with Wh-Questions 87

7.12 Think Fast! Practicing Verb Tenses.................................. 88

7.18 When Suddenly... 94

10. LOW BEGINNERS

Most of the activities in this book are easily adapted for the full range of beginning students. You can use them with low beginners if you control content and vocabulary. We have indexed here those activities that are already suitable for low-beginning students.

1.6   Checking the Weather 4

1.9   What Day Is It Today? 6

2.8   Picture Dictation 17

3.4   What's Your Name? Nice to Meet You 23

3.5   Please and Thank You 23

5.1   Let's Learn Those Letters 42

5.2   Fill-in-the-Blank Dictation.. 43

5.5   The Appearing and Disappearing Sentence 46

5.9   Spelling Improvement.. 51

6.1   Classic Total Physical Response (TPR): Actions Tell the Story 54

6.3   TPR: Working with Money 57

6.9   All the Words We Know.. 63

6.11 Alphabet on the Wall: Collecting Words.......................................65

6.14 Playing with Numbers: What Adds Up to 14? 68

6.15 Playing with Numbers: Students Make Their Own Equations 69

7.5   Substitution Drills 80

11. MOVEMENT

Students have more fun and remember language better when it's anchored by movement. Even standing up to mingle or manipulating objects counts as movement!

1.3   Dance Party 3

1.7   Taking Surveys 5

2.1   Popcorn Listening 10

2.4   Let's Pack a Suitcase 13

2.5   Active True/False 14

3.7   Let's Put on a Play! 26

3.8   Homework or Quiz Review: Seek and Find 27

4.2   On the Wall Outside 31

5.1   Let's Learn Those Letters 42

6.1   Classic Total Physical Response (TPR): Actions Tell the Story 54

6.2   TPR: Making a Peanut Butter Sandwich 6

6.3   TPR: Working with Money 57

6.10 Manipulating Objects or Pictures 64

6.11 Alphabet on the Wall: Collecting Words 65

6.13 The Hokey Pokey 67

6.15 Playing with Numbers: Students Make Their Own Equations 69

6.19 What Am I Drawing? 72

7.1   Tell It Like It Isn't 76

7.6   Truth or Chair? 81

7.11 Playing with Wh-Questions 87

12. MULTIPLE INTELLIGENCES

See the following index categories: Drawing, Movement, Music and Song, and Pictures.

13. MUSIC AND SONG

People remember the language they learn in songs, and the pleasure of songs increases motivation.

1.3   Dance Party 3

2.2   Singing Dictation: Building Up a Song 11

6.13 The Hokey Pokey 67

14. PICTURES

One picture is worth a thousand words to beginners. Pictures make the meaning clear when words alone are not enough. The following activities use pictures.

2.4   Let's Pack a Suitcase 13

3.9   Reconstruct the Story 22

4.2   On the Wall Outside 31

4.8   Predicting from the Picture 37

6.4   From Pictures to Words 58

6.8   Half a Picture 62

6.12 Two Unrelated Pictures: How Are They the Same? 66

7.9   Cleaning Up the Mess 85

15. POLITE PHRASES

These are the first things people need in a new language

1.1   Hello! How are you? (Greetings) 2

2.7   Catch the Teacher's Mistakes (Polite Correction) 16

3.4   What's Your Name? Nice to Meet You! (Introductions)................. 23

3.5   Please and Thank You (Asking permission/showing gratitude) 23

16. PREVIEW

Too often, we ask students to do two things at the same time: decipher words and process the meaning of a listening or reading passage. For all levels, and especially for beginners, this can be too challenging! When we pre-teach the meaning in advance, students listen and read with real pleasure and satisfaction. These activities help students stay excited about learning their new language.

2.8   Picture Dictation 17

4.3   Dictocomp: Rewriting from Key Words 33

4.5   New Words and What They Mean 35

4.7   Predicting from the Title 37

4.8   Predicting from the Picture 37

6.16 What We Already Know About This............................... 70

17. PRONUNCIATION

Many of the activities in this book can be used to focus on pronunciation. Here are a few that have pronunciation as a primary focus.

2.2   Singing Dictation: Building Up a Song 11

2.9   Gossip 18

3.7   Let's Put on a Play! 26

4.2   On the Wall Outside 31

4.4   Students Choose Who's Next 34

18. REVIEW

Recycling language is essential for beginners. It must be done with variety so that their interest remains high. Here are some activities for effective review.

1.9   What Day Is It Today? 6

2.5   Active True/False 14

2.6   Who Said It? 15

4.1   Let's Make it False 30

4.3   Dictocomp: Rewriting from Key Words 33

4.6   Add a Picture 36

19. SETTLING DOWN THE CLASS

Try these activities if your students need to settle down and focus their attention.

1.8   Offering Tea 6

1.10 What Can We Hear 7

4.6   Add a Picture 36

5.10 One-Minute Feedback 51

20. SHORT ACTIVITIES

Are you waiting for a few late students? Do you have a few extra minutes at the end of a class? Try these!

1.2   Early Bird Questions 2

1.3   Dance Party 3

1.6   Checking the Weather 4

1.10 What Can We Hear? 7

5.9   Spelling Improvement 51

6.7   Vocabulary Cards 61

21. SPELLING

Any number of activities can be used to reinforce spelling. Here are a few to consider.

2.2   Singing Dictation: Building Up a Song 11

3.8   Homework or Quiz Review: Seek and Find 27

5.3   Let's Find Some Useful Mistakes 44

5.9   Spelling Improvement 51

6.7   Vocabulary Cards 61

22. STUDENTS HELPING STUDENTS

You'll find many activities have students working sometimes in pairs or groups. With well-designed activities, even beginners can support one another's learning.

1.4   One New Word 3

1.10 What Can We Hear? 7

3.2   What I Need 21

3.8   Homework or Quiz Review: Seek and Find 27

4.2   On the Wall Outside 31

4.9   Telling Back and Forth 38

5.7   Partners in Writing 48

6.20 Student-Run Vocabulary Review 73

23. STUDENTS IN CHARGE OF THEIR OWN LEARNING

With the right support, even beginners can work independently. Here are some activities that build confidence and give students pride in their own abilities.

1.2   Early Bird Questions 2

1.4   One New Word 3

2.3   Using the Telephone 12

3.1   Classroom Language 20

3.2   What I Need 21

3.8   Homework or Quiz Review: Seek and Find 27

5.6   The Vocabulary of Sentences and Paragraphs 46

5.7   Partners in Writing 48

5.8   Editing and Revision: I Can Do It Myself 49

5.10 One-Minute Feedback 51

6.7   Vocabulary Cards 61

6.18 Use it Before I Sleep 72

24. VOCABULARY CATEGORIES

Here are some activities that target a specific set of words and other activities that use a vocabulary set as an example but are equally good for teaching other words.

Alphabet

5.1   Let's Learn Those Letters 42

6.11 Alphabet on the Wall: Collecting Words..................... 65

Body parts

6.13 The Hokey Pokey 67

Colors

2.4   Let's Pack a Suitcase 13

7.17 Vocabulary Chain (variation)................................... 93

Foods

3.9   What I Eat, What You Eat 28

7.7   Building Dialogues About Food 83

Household Items

2.4   Let's Pack a Suitcase 13

7.9   Cleaning Up the Mess.. 85

Money

6.3   TPR: Working with Money 57

Months of the Year

1.9   What Day Is It Today? 6

6.6   Getting to Know You: A Birthday Game 60

Numbers

1.9   What Day Is It Today? 6

2.3   Using the Telephone 12

6.3   TPR: Working with Money 57

6.5   Practicing Counting 59

6.6   Getting to Know You: A Birthday Game 60

6.14 Playing with Numbers: What Adds Up to 14? 68

6.15 Playing with Numbers: Students Make Their Own Equations 69

Personal Items

1.5   What's in My Wallet? 4

2.4   Let's Pack a Suitcase 13

Real Objects

1.5   What's in My Wallet? 4

6.3   TPR: Working with Money 57

7.6   Truth or Chair?.. 81

7.13 This is My Elephant 89

Seasons and Weather

1.6   Checking the Weather 4

1.9   What Day Is It Today? 6

ALPHABETICAL INDEX OF ACTIVITIES

Do you remember the name of an activity but not the chapter you found it in? This list is for you!

2.5	Active True/False	14
4.6	Add a Picture	36
6.9	All the Words We Know	63
6.11	Alphabet on the Wall: Collecting Words	65
7.7	Building Dialogues About Food	83
2.7	Catch the Teacher's Mistakes	16
5.4	Chain Story	45
1.6	Checking the Weather	4
6.1	Classic Total Physical Response (TPR): Actions Tell the Story	54
3.1	Classroom Language	20
7.9	Cleaning Up the Mess	85
6.21	Creating New Stories with Our Words	74
1.3	Dance Party	3
4.3	Dictocomp: Rewriting from Key Words	33
1.2	Early Bird Questions	2
5.8	Editing and Revision: I Can Do It Myself	49
5.2	Fill-in the-Blank Dictation	43
6.17	Four Corners Vocabulary	71
6.4	From Pictures to Words	58
6.6	Getting to Know You: A Birthday Game	60
2.9	Gossip	18
6.8	Half a Picture	62
1.1	Hello! How Are You?	2
3.8	Homework or Quiz Review: Seek and Find	27
5.3	Let's Find Some Useful Mistakes	44
5.1	Let's Learn Those Letters	42
4.1	Let's Make It False	30

2.4   Let's Pack a Suitcase 13

3.7   Let's Put on a Play! 26

7.2   Make Questions for the Answers 77

6.10 Manipulating Objects or Pictures 64

4.5   New Words and What They Mean 35

1.8   Offering Tea 6

4.2   On the Wall Outside 31

1.4   One New Word 3

5.10 One-Minute Feedback 51

5.7   Partners in Writing 48

2.8   Picture Dictation 17

6.15 Playing with Numbers: Students Make Their Own Equations 69

6.14 Playing with Numbers: What Adds Up to 14? 68

7.11 Playing with Wh-Questions 87

3.5   Please and Thank You 23

2.1   Popcorn Listening 10

6.5   Practicing Counting 59

4.8   Predicting from the Picture 37

4.7   Predicting from the Title 37

7.15 Preposition Pictures 91

3.6   Reading and Speaking 3 x 3 24

3.3   Reconstruct the Story 22

7.16 Scrambling Words in a Sentence 92

7.4   Sentence Contraction 79

7.3   Sentence Expansion 78

2.2   Singing Dictation: Building Up a Song 11

5.9   Spelling Improvement 51

6.20 Student-Run Vocabulary Review 73

4.4   Students Choose Who's Next 34

7.5   Substitution Drills 80

1.7   Taking Surveys 5

7.1   Tell It Like It Isn't 76

4.9   Telling Back and Forth 38

5.5   The Appearing and Disappearing Sentence 46

6.13 The Hokey Pokey 67

5.6   The Vocabulary of Sentences and Paragraphs 46

7.12 Think Fast! Practicing Verb Tenses 88

7.13 This is My Elephant 89

6.2   TPR: Making a Peanut Butter Sandwich 56

6.3   TPR: Working with Money 57

7.6   Truth or Chair? 81

6.12 Two Unrelated Pictures: How Are They the Same? 66

6.18 Use it Before I Sleep 72

2.3   Using the Telephone 12

6.7   Vocabulary Cards 61

7.17 Vocabulary Chain 93

7.14 Weekly Routines 90

6.19 What Am I Drawing? 72

1.10 What Can We Hear? 7

1.9   What Day Is It Today? 6

7.8   What Do We Do? Practicing Short Answers with Do and Does 84

3.9   What I Eat, What You Eat 28

3.2   What I Need 21

7.10 What Kind of Noun is This? 86

6.16 What We Already Know About This 70

1.5   What's in My Wallet? 4

3.4   What's Your Name? Nice to Meet You! 23

7.18 When Suddenly 94

2.6   Who Said It? 15